MANAGEMENT OF
INFORMATION SYSTEMS CASEBOOK

MANAGEMENT OF INFORMATION SYSTEMS CASEBOOK

Gary W. Dickson

University of Minnesota

James C. Wetherbe

University of Minnesota

McGraw-Hill Book Company

New York   St. Louis   San Francisco   Auckland   Bogotá   Hamburg
Johannesburg   London   Madrid   Mexico   Montreal   New Delhi
Panama   Paris   São Paulo   Singapore   Sydney   Tokyo   Toronto

To Katherine A. Cooper

This book was set in Press Roman by The Whitlock Press, Inc.
The editors were Christina Mediate and Joseph F. Murphy; the
cover was designed by Suzanne Haldane; the production
supervisor was Marietta Breitwieser.
R. R. Donnelley & Sons Company was printer and binder.

MANAGEMENT OF INFORMATION SYSTEMS CASEBOOK

ISBN 0-07-016827-X

1234567890 DOC DOC 898765

Library of Congress Cataloging in Publication Data

Dickson, Gary W.
    Management of information systems casebook.

(McGraw-Hill series in management information
systems)
    1. Management information systems—Management—
Case studies.   I. Wetherbe, James C.   II. Title.
III. Series.
T58.6.D46   1985   658.4'0388   85-5187
ISBN 0-07-016827-X

CONTENTS

The *Management of Information Systems Casebook* contains a variety of cases dealing with topics frequently encountered by information systems managers. Planning, staffing, equipment selection, and "people" problems are but a few examples of topics involved in the cases in this book. In writing the cases, the authors have used their extensive experience in dealing with real organizations to construct situations that are typical of those with which the contemporary information systems manager will have to deal.

The cases in this book tend to focus on the problem areas of the IS manager or subordinate managers in the IS function. Thus the focus of this book is not on issues typically dealt with by executive management, e.g., strategic uses of information systems or the level of resources to devote to the IS function. Because of the focus, the audience for this book is in a capstone course for information systems specialists or involved in a depth course in information systems. Ideally, the book supports our book *The Management of Information Systems* but may be used with other more basic information systems texts.

Many of the cases in this book are relatively short. Because of this fact, cases can be used in class sessions along with topical discussions or can be read in class prior to discussion. Longer cases, e.g., Perigee Industries, are typically broken into parts that build on each other. Normally, multipart cases require a part to be read or worked before work can commence on the next part. Cases requiring depth analysis prior to their discussion are noted in the Instructor's Manual.

In real life, problems do not come labeled "I am a problem dealing with people's resistance to change," or "I am a problem of estimating the computer's future processing capacity." For this reason, the cases in this book are arranged alphabetically so that students have to determine what problem or problems are present in the situation described and draw from different sources or chapters in their text to come up with solutions. To assist the instructor in assigning cases, the major focus of each case is stated in the Instructor's Manual. Assignments are given at the conclusion of each case, but the instructor may modify these or give completely different assignments.

To preserve confidences, all the case names are fictitious and geographical locations have been changed. In some instances, all the facts are authentic, while in some others the facts have been disguised by changing the data so as not to alter the basic relationships. Several cases are built upon facts from two or many actual situations.

Analysis of a case may reveal that some of the data given may be superfluous to the particular problem in the case or that additional data which would be desirable to have are not provided. This is typical of complicated situations involved in the management of information systems and tests the manager's ability to select the pertinent data from large quantities of data, much of which may not be relevant. It also tests the manager's ability to make plausible assumptions about other factors which are relevant but unavailable or unknown. Many of the cases will have alternative solutions. The best analytical approach will be to

compare numerous feasible courses of action and to recognize
that many decisions must be made with incomplete knowledge
about all the relevant factors. Often there will be a lack
of unanimous agreement among the students in determining the
most workable solution. Differences of opinion are valuable
because they lead to a better understanding of the problem,
the general concepts that are involved, and the many inter-
relationships affecting the solution.

In writing this casebook, the authors directed their
efforts toward situations in information systems management
that are common and of the type frequently encountered by
information systems managers. It is our hope that the
student will find these situations interesting, stimulating
and useful.

Gary W. Dickson
James C. Wetherbe

Acme Guaranteed Builders is one of three divisions of Zenith Architects. The architectural division is by far the largest of the three, but Acme has been the glamour division in the past few years because of its very high profit rate. Acme is in the business of bidding fixed-price contracts for buildings, financing them, subcontracting the architectural work to Zenith's architectural division, and doing the construction. For the past several years, Acme's primary activity has been in the construction of hospitals (including major expansions) and hotel/motels.

All the corporate computing used by the divisions and the parent organization is provided by a centralized data processing organization which developed application programs using PL/1 and run on the firm's 4331-11. (See Figure 1 for Acme's fit in Zenith's organizational structure and for the location of the DP activity.) Virtually all the computer applications could be classified as being the business type, but an abortive attempt had been made to use a special-purpose computer for assisting the architects. Because of technical difficulties, this activity was very limited, and most of the time this machine was sitting idle.

In the summer of 1983, the president of Acme was very dissatisfied with the computer support (or lack thereof) he was getting from the central DP organization. In effect, it

1

Figure 1 Acme Guaranteed Builders:
organization structure

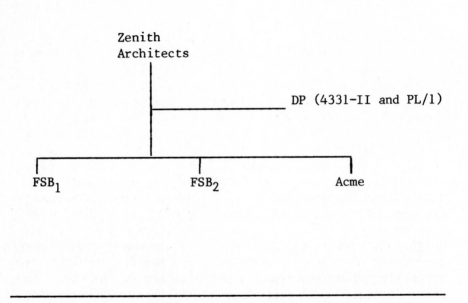

had failed to respond to his requests to provide a computer application to assist Acme's project cost control.   For several months, Parker Biggs, the manager of project cost control, had been trying to work with one of DP's seven analysts to design and implement a cost control system for the various construction projects.   Over this time, much discussion had taken place and a number of meetings had been held, but the system was apparently no closer to realization than it had been several months earlier.

   One of the reasons for the president's dissatisfaction was his feeling that it was critical to Acme's business success that it estimate project costs accurately in the bidding process and then carefully monitor actual costs during the construction phase.   He was heard to say that for a business doing business on a fixed-price basis the most critical thing to do well was to control the project costs. He knew that, from the present level of four active projects underway around the country in the summer of 1983, the company was likely to have as many as three times that many going by the summer of 1984. Most of these, in addition, would be run by project managers new to the company, and the combination of increased business activity and new project managers was an invitation to financial disaster unless a standard computer-based cost control system was in place early in 1984. Time, he felt, was running out on implementing such a system.

With this situation in mind, the president and Acme's vice president of finance decided to honor Parker Biggs's request to be allowed to attend a 3-day executive program run by a local university on the subject of "building effective information systems." If one were to categorize the Acme president as dissatisfied with the service given by Zenith's DP organization and anxious about the future, then Biggs's feelings were about 10 times stronger than those of the president. Biggs had the frustration of trying to work with the central DP analyst and the disappointment of getting absolutely nowhere. Further, as manager of the company's cost control, he was absolutely convinced of the need for a computer-based cost control system to handle the anticipated new construction projects. He felt that without such a system neither he nor the project managers could do their jobs. It was with this background that he became aware of the university's executive program, which promised to show users how to get effective information systems. He thought that maybe this program would help him find a way of getting the project cost control system he so desperately needed.

The program was everything Biggs expected, and more. The program emphasized MIS system planning, its importance, how to do it, and the role of the user. Biggs got so turned on that after the program, he took 2 days of vacation plus a weekend and developed a 55-page MIS plan for Acme. In addition, he prioritized the systems he identified and detailed what the project cost control system would produce and how this system would work from a user perspective. He then submitted the plan to his boss, Acme's vice president of finance, and to the firm's president.

These two managers were very impressed. They agreed on the plan and its detail but had difficulty when considering the next step. They felt that they were now secure in knowing what they wanted to do with information systems but were very uncomfortable about how to go about doing it. In particular, they were uncomfortable with taking the plan to Zenith's DP manager. First, they felt that he would reject the plan because it was developed by users, not by DP personnel, and because it was "not invented here." Second, they felt that since the central DP organization had done nothing for the past 7 months there was little likelihood this situation would change in the future. Biggs decided to contact one of the two professors who had conducted the program he had attended and see if he could be hired to help get a system in place in a time frame consistent with what all three managers thought was Acme's critical need.

VENDOR SELECTION

Professor Johnson agreed to assist Acme Guaranteed Builders with obtaining a project cost control system. In late September, he met with the president of the company and Parker Biggs. They agreed that the task at hand was to (1) review the MIS plan developed by Biggs, (2) given an adequate plan, develop a request for proposal and contact a few vendors judged to be capable of having a working system available by late January 1984, and (3) make a decision as to whether one of these vendors should be selected to provide the system and, if so, which one.

Professor Johnson suggested that given the very tight time schedule, a limited number of vendors be considered and at least two of these use what he called "nontraditional" languages. He explained that there were now available computer languages, called very high level languages, that offered a great deal of power over a traditional language like PL/1. This, he suggested, would greatly increase the chances of meeting the president's condition that a system be available by late January. Johnson emphasized the fact that the Acme project control system, as well as other, lower-priority systems, did not rely on any of Zenith's central computer applications or data and thus were good candidates for systems developed according to what he called a "prototype" design strategy.

Johnson and Biggs worked together to develop a letter to send to three vendors describing the time constraints to develop the system and to convey the fact that a copy of the system plan was enclosed. A steering committee for the project was established. Members were the Acme president, the Acme vice president of finance, Biggs, Johnson, Zenith's head accountant, the Acme manager to whom all the construction project managers reported, and the Acme manager responsible for project estimating. The charge given to the steering committee was to participate in listening to the vendor presentations and to make, as a group, the vendor selection decision.

The president stated that one of the "vendors" in the final group from whom the selection would be made would be the central Zenith DP organization. He noted that he had little faith that it could develop the system in the time needed (given its past track record), but for political reasons it had to be considered. With the internal Zenith DP organization considered as vendor A, letters were sent to vendors, B, C, and D to see if they would be interested in bidding on developing the system. The letter instructed the vendors that Acme was interested in a fixed-price contract for the system. All three vendors asked to be allowed to gather more information from Acme and to be allowed to bid on the system. The vendors, then, were as follows:

Vendor A. The Zenith DP organization. It would assign a systems analyst to work with Biggs, and the system would be developed in PL/1 and would run on Zenith's IBM 4331. The Acme office was about 3 miles from the Zenith office and data center, so the plan was for CRT/printer stations to be located in the Acme office and communicate at 9600 bps with the Zenith computer.

Vendor B. A very high quality national software firm with a very large staff located in the same city as Acme and Zenith. It would put two analysts on the project and would contract out the programming, which would be in PL/1. The application would be run on Zenith's 4331, and the equipment in the Acme office would be the same as described above.

Vendor C. The local branch of a very well known national time-sharing company. The application would be developed in Focus and run on a time-sharing system with two terminals (CRT and printers) in the Acme office. Two local analysts would work on the design and programming of the system with the technical assistance of a Focus "expert" out of the firm's Chicago office.

Vendor D. A company proposing advanced database-oriented software run on IBM PC/XTs. This company was located in a small town about 100 miles from Acme's headquarters. It was a relatively new firm with about 15 employees and would assign its best applications programmer to the development and implementation of the Acme project cost control system.

From September until early November 1983, each of the vendors met frequently with Biggs, Johnson, and other Acme personnel to firm up the system specifications and design. During this period, the system became Biggs's full-time job. In the second week of November, each of the vendors made a lengthy presentation to the steering committee detailing how it would develop the system, the time frame for system operation, and its costs. Figure 2 summarizes the proposals.

Note in Figure 2 that the vendors bid the cost of developing the system (a one-time cost), the cost of operating the system for a year, and the time at which the developed system would be available. Several comments are in order. First, vendor B would not guarantee a fixed price for the systems development. The $95,000 figure is an estimate based upon time and materials. If forced to make a fixed quote, vendor B said it would do it for twice the price it estimated although it fully believed it would come in at a figure consistent with that estimated. Further, the operating cost for vendor B was taken to be the same as that developed by the in-house DP organization since there was no basis to assume differently. The operational cost of vendor C on time-sharing was quoted to be a monthly figure of approximately the same magnitude of annual expenses on the in-house computer.

The price bid by vendor D is difficult to compare since the price is a one-time charge for two microcomputer systems. The only ongoing charge was for maintenance. In

Figure 2 Costs and schedules

	Traditional			Nontraditional
	A	B	C	D
Cost:				
Development	$35,000	$95,000	$35,000	$7000
Operation	$7000 per year	$7000 per year	$6000 per month	$26,000* + $300 per month
Time	6 months	5 months	3 months	6 weeks
Qualitative factor score	89.6	121.6	172.5	179.4

*One-time charge and monthly maintenance.

terms of time performance, vendor D promised the system in mid-January, vendor C by the end of February, vendor B by the end of April, and vendor A by the end of May.

A subcommittee of the steering committee, Johnson, Biggs, and the Zenith head accountant, developed a system in which various vendor attributes and their bids were weighted to arrive at a vendor "score." The group went through this exercise and arrived at the following scores, which were presented to the steering committee prior to its decision-making session: vendor A = 89.6, vendor B = 121.6, vendor C = 172.5, and vendor D = 179.4. It is fair to note that vendor A's low rating was affected by the bad experience Acme had had with the internal data processing group at Zenith. There was little belief on the part of Biggs and other Acme managers that this bid was accurate.

At the session of the steering committee devoted to making a decision, the process was reviewed and each vendor's detailed bids were presented. At the conclusion of the presentation, the Acme president took about 10 seconds to observe that vendor D was the clear option. He said that he could afford to make the investment in the systems development and if in about 6 weeks the system did not work out, start over. He further observed that the project management system, if it saved one costly error, would recover the $33,000 investment very quickly.

Acme immediately signed a contract with vendor D to develop the project management cost control system. Acme, in notifying vendors B and C of the contract decision, stated how impressed it was with their quality and professionalism. They were told they would be recontacted should the chosen alternative not work out. In fact, a decision was made to select vendor C should vendor D be unable to perform in the 6 weeks following the selection decision.

ASSIGNMENT

Write a report critiquing the selection of a vendor to provide Acme Guaranteed Builders with a system to control its construction project costs. In your report consider:

1. Was the selection process sound? If not, what were the major weaknesses?
2. Comment on the ability of Acme to "go its own way," bypassing the central data processing organization. How might a more synergistic approach have been taken?
3. What about the emphasis on a "nontraditional approach"? Was Johnson wise to suggest this approach and to some extent "push" its consideration?
4. In many ways, vendor C was the most professional of the bidders and, to some extent, the safe alternative. Its very high cost of systems operation caused it not to be selected. Comment on this situation.

The vendor selected to develop a project cost control system for Acme Guaranteed Builders was Probe Systems, a firm about 1 year old that had developed a very good database system and an associated procedural processor for the IBM PC/XT. As was mentioned in Part A, Probe Systems was headquartered in a small town about 100 miles from Acme. Probe Systems assigned their best applications programmer, Bill Lieffer, to the Acme contract.

Lieffer knew that finishing the system by the end of January 1984 was very important. He had been instrumental in preparing Probe's bid and was confident that the MEGA-FIELD system developed by Probe would allow him to prototype the system and meet the deadline. His experience with other applications had, in some cases, yielded compression of as much as 65 to 1 from COBOL to MEGAFIELD.

Between the signing of the contract and the first of the year, Lieffer and Biggs worked almost full time on the design and coding of the project cost control system. By the first week in January, a preliminary version of the system was available for demonstration to a group composed of the Acme president, Professor Johnson, and the head accountant from Zenith Architects. They were very impressed. At the meeting at which the demonstration was given, several further system enhancements were suggested, with Biggs and

Lieffer agreeing that the improvements could be incorporated in the system by the end of January.

By the third week in January, the project cost control system was completed, and the data from a first project, a hotel being built in Michigan, was being entered into the system. As soon as the data was entered, certain shortcomings in the design of the system were noted. Lieffer stated that he had fulfilled the original contract specifications and would need additional funding to enhance the system according to the newly identified requirements. The Acme president approved a new contract, at a cost almost as much as that of the original one, to more fully develop the system.

While Lieffer was programming and Biggs was working with him on design and testing, Acme's business was growing rapidly. From a base of three operational construction projects, contracts were signed for five more. Managers to handle the new projects were being hired while, at the same time, some of the existing projects were in trouble. In the latter cases, either construction was behind schedule or there was the feeling that costs were out of line. Two project managers were hired from outside Acme to replace those who were not doing so well. It is a practice in the construction industry to have very high turnover in the position of project manager. Professor Johnson once admitted that as one unfamiliar with this industry, he almost needed a program to tell who was working for whom at any point.

In the spring of 1984, Probe Systems decided to open a major sales office in the city in which Acme was located. The Acme office manager knew of space in the same building in which Acme was renting space and suggested to Bill Lieffer that this space might meet Probe's requirements in that it was about the right size and located near the airport. After some negotiation, Probe leased this space and had a sales office located right next to what it considered to be one of its major customers. At about the same time, Professor Johnson was engaged to reexamine the Acme systems plan developed almost a year ago and work with Acme personnel to update the plan and to begin working on a detailed design of a project estimating system.

In June 1984, the situation at Acme was becoming critical. Several major projects were underway in Florida and needed managerial control on site. The Acme vice president of finance, Biggs's boss, was sent to Florida to head up a major office closer to those projects. Meanwhile, as the data for new projects was being added to the project cost control system, more system shortcomings were found, and further system changes (and costs) were incurred.

On July 1, 1984, Parker Biggs was sent by Acme to Florida to become a project manager on a construction site. He moved with his family to become a resident of that state. On July 15, 1984, the Acme president suspended all activity on the project cost control system and said the PC/XT would be used to support word processing by the secretarial staff. He stated that the system took too much trouble to get the data in and keep it up to date and that unless this was done, the systems outputs were useless. Finally, he said he was convinced that the project managers, other than Parker Biggs, would not take the trouble to submit timely and accurate data and would not use the system to manage their projects. "They're too busy managing their projects to worry about collecting data for a system that is supposed to help them manage their projects," he concluded.

ASSIGNMENT

Here we have a situation which, in one sense, was a technical success. The system was developed on time and produced what the customer said it wanted. Even when the customer "learned" and generated new requirements, the software was flexible and powerful enough to quickly respond. Still, the system was not used.

1. What was the major cause of Acme giving up on the system for controlling project costs?

2. What could have been done to prevent this outcome?

3. How can a balance be struck so that a user gets a system it wants but at some time the system comes to an end and constant evolution stops? In one sense, a very high level language like MEGAFIELD helps this situation in that it is relatively easy to change, but in another sense the flexibility is a disadvantage. Explain.

Better Merchandising, Inc., is a Chicago-based direct marketing company. It has been in existence since the late 1920s and has enjoyed reasonable success during its existence. Better Merchandising made an early entry into computer-based information systems in the early 1960s. During the early years of automation, it was extremely progressive, always successfully implementing the latest technology.

By the early 1970s, Better Merchandising was nationally recognized as one of the leaders in the use of computer-based information systems. It had been written up in several national business journals, and its information systems management was often asked to give workshops and presentations on how information systems had been developed at Better Merchandising.

As a result of the success of Better Merchandising's information systems, many other organizations continually attempted to recruit both its information systems management and its technical staff. Over a period of years leading up to the mid-1970s, the top talent at Better Merchandising was pirated away by other corporations.

The management at Better Merchandising was quite content with its information systems and saw little reason to panic at the loss of staff. The less-ambitious and generally less-talented staff that remained did a reasonable job of maintaining the information systems developed in the late 1960s and early 1970s that created Better Merchandising's reputation.

By the early 1980s, the world had passed Better Merchandising by in the area of information systems. Better Merchandising staff, having primarily focused on maintaining systems that were developed over a decade ago, had put little effort into developing new leading-edge information systems. As a result, they had done little in the areas of database and integrated systems, distributed data processing, decision support systems, and end-user computing. Their information systems generally had minimal strategic impact on the few development projects that had been undertaken.

In a 1982 general shake-up of top management, a new president, Mr. Paul Annett, was recruited from a New York department store chain. Mr. Annett's complete evaluation of Better Merchandising emphasized the deterioration of the information systems function. Mr. Annett was known for the leadership role he had played in making information systems effective at his previous firm.

After having in-depth discussions with the key information systems managers currently at Better Merchandising, Mr. Annett concluded that to turn around the information systems effort would require new leadership. He therefore hired an executive search firm to find him a capable, leading-edge information executive.

After an extensive national search, David Johnson, an information systems manager with a small Cincinnati firm, was hired. Mr. Johnson had done a phenomenal job of turning around the information systems function at his previous organization.

After coming on board, Mr. Johnson immediately started making changes. He assessed information systems staff and realized that they had become quite obsolete in terms of skills and orientation. He also realized that he was understaffed to take on the new projects Mr. Annett was proposing.

Mr. Johnson immediately went on a national search to hire 12 first-rate MBAs in MIS out of top-notch schools. Having successfully recruited these graduates, he began to spread them among the different information systems activities

within the IS function. He also began to recruit two direct
reports to serve on his immediate staff. He was able to
bring in Jan Hadley as a systems development manager and Ed
Rubenstein to head up production. Both people were exceptionally talented, with good work records in management.

Mr. Johnson quickly became entangled in a variety of
complex corporate issues involving end-user computing, information systems planning, and steering committees. At the
end of a year, much to Mr. Johnson's surprise, 3 of his 12
newly hired MBAs had left Better Merchandising. Word
through the grapevine indicated that all the new MBAs were
quite dissatisfied with their new positions and were looking
for other employment opportunities.

Alarmed and concerned, Mr. Johnson called a meeting of
the remaining "new" MBAs to discuss their feelings about
their jobs. However, he was able to get little meaningful
information as to what the problem was. The MBAs tended to
talk in vague generalities and provided little specific
information as to what their concerns were, though it was
clear that something was troubling them.

Mr. Johnson discussed the problem with Ms. Hadley and Mr.
Rubenstein, who suggested they might get more candid information from the three individuals who had already left
Better Merchandising. Mr. Johnson followed up on this idea
and was able to get some straightforward information. The
former employees indicated that at Better Merchandising they
had all been placed in a reporting relationship to people
who were not that progressive about their jobs and not
supportive of the new leadership in the MIS organization.
In fact, they had felt resented by their supervisors and
ostracized by other employees in the department. They were
convinced of the progressive and innovative thinking of the
leadership of the MIS department, but being buried a couple
of layers below that leadership, they felt like there was
very little hope for advancement for them in the foreseeable
future. After about a year's worth of frustration, they
decided that their career interests would be better served
by leaving Better Merchandising.

Mr. Johnson was surprised by this information and immediately shared it with Ms. Hadley and Mr. Rubenstein. After
careful thought, they decided the explanation of the former
employees did make sense. The managers agreed that they had
felt some "passive" resistance from their immediate subor-

dinates to whom the new MBAs reported and did not feel they were getting as much support as they should from the new regime. It was easy to understand that this resistance would be much more direct and conspicuous to newly hired employees who were in a much weaker political position than were the managers.

Mr. Johnson, Ms. Hadley, and Mr. Rubenstein followed up this meeting with individual meetings with the remaining MBAs. They directly asked, though with some finesse, the remaining MBAs if they felt somewhat stymied in their progress, or if they were not comfortable with the support level they were getting from their immediate supervision. At this point, most of the MBAs really opened up and shared their feelings similar to those of the employees who had left Better Merchandising.

After reviewing the results of their meetings with the MBAs, Mr. Johnson, Ms. Hadley, and Mr. Rubenstein felt they really had a handle on the problem. The staff left over from the former regime was clearly creating a problem with the newly hired MBAs. The new management wanted to be supportive and encourage the new MBAs, but they also felt that they had to be supportive to the layer of management between them and those employees. The problem was to find a strategy to solve the problem.

ASSIGNMENT

1. What positive steps can Mr. Johnson, Ms. Hadley, and Mr. Rubenstein take to solve this problem? You can assume that most of the previous staff at Better Merchandising do not have MBAs and are somewhat intimidated, feeling that they might not have credentials that are competitive with newly hired employees.

2. If your first strategy was not successful, what would be your second approach?

Linda Schroeder was recently appointed MIS vice president for Commercial Insurance Company. Ms. Schroeder has extensive information management background, having started out as a programmer 18 years ago and holding progressively responsible positions, including systems analyst, operations director, director of technical services, and manager of information systems development, prior to joining Commercial Insurance. Her work experience has primarily been with financial institutions, including one bank, two savings and loans, and one other insurance company.

Commercial Insurance is a holding company for several commercial insurance enterprises. Its annual revenue is in excess of $1.2 billion. It has made extensive use of computer systems in handling its financial transactions and until 5 years ago had had reasonable success with its systems. However, since 1980 there has been a slow deterioration in the quality of its systems and the quality of staff used to develop them.

In early 1984, a lot of negative sentiment developed toward the then MIS manager, Mr. Ronald Hickman. This negative sentiment reached a peak in late 1984 when top management called for an audit of the information systems department. The audit was to include both a controls assessment and a performance assessment. A "Big Eight" account-

17

ing firm was hired to perform the audit and was generally made aware of top management's negative attitude toward the information systems department. The audit team found several problems with the information systems department in both the control and the performance area. Having sensed a hidden agenda to discredit the information systems manager, the auditors did not pull any punches in their quite unflattering review of the information systems department.

The top management used the information from the audit report as grounds for terminating Mr. Hickman. Mr. Hickman appealed his case and having a couple of contacts on the board of directors, he made special arguments to them, hoping they could intercede on his behalf. The members of the board of directors did raise the issue at a meeting; however, the decision to terminate Mr. Hickman was confirmed.

There were no internal candidates to replace Mr. Hickman, so Commercial Insurance conducted a national search for a new vice president of information systems. Linda Schroeder was the unanimous selection of top management and was hired in early 1985.

During the interview, the top management of Commercial Insurance did not really reveal the extent to which its information systems had deteriorated. Ms. Schroeder did ask to meet with several of the staff of the information systems function; however, top management declined to let her have such access. Their argument was that there was an internal candidate for the position and they did not want to create any sudden resignations by having people get upset by the possibility of bringing someone in from the outside to fill the key management position. This argument sounded reasonable to Ms. Schroeder and she accepted it.

During the interview, top management indicated the desire to move forward with all their existing systems to an on-line, database environment making use of personal computers in a distributed fashion to offload processing as much as possible out to the end-user. This strategy sounded reasonable to Ms. Schroeder, and she agreed that it was conceptually feasible. She even went so far as to say that their major applications could be moved into this environment within a $1\frac{1}{2}$- to 2-year time frame, with the most critical systems being converted during the first year.

Her first day on the job Ms. Schroeder arrived in her new office to find sitting at the center of her desk a copy of the audit report prepared by the "Big Eight" accounting firm. Reading through it, she became quite distressed by the many difficulties in the department and with its systems. General findings were as follows:

Staff is inadequately trained and unfamiliar with advanced concepts and techniques for developing systems.
Information systems are dated and aren't using state-of-the-art technology.
Existing systems are not documented and, if key staff should leave, would unlikely be able to be supported should any changes be required.
Virtually all systems are lacking in adequate controls; a major error could go undetected in many of the systems.
Backup and recovery procedures are totally inadequate. Loss of key files of computing facilities would undoubtedly be disastrous to the survival of Commercial Insurance.
Computer security is totally inadequate. Unauthorized personnel have easy access to the machine room and sensitive data.
Performance of existing software is significantly inefficient, resulting in enormous waste of computer time.
Users are totally dissatisfied with the support they have received for their information systems. Major complaints include systems reports usually being late and often requiring reruns to correct errors.
Users complain that information systems staff is insensitive and unresponsive to their needs, showing little cooperation to help users with major problems.

After reviewing the document and recovering from the initial shock, Ms. Schroeder visited with some of her senior information systems staff and asked them what they thought about the audit. They, in general, concurred with the findings of the audit, though they felt that the staff was presented in the most negative light possible. During these discussion, Ms. Schroeder found out that her predecessor had been terminated after a rather nasty battle. She had been led to believe during her interview that her predecessor's leaving had been mutually agreed upon.

To make matters worse, the next day she was called to a meeting with Mr. Bob Lightheuser, executive vice president, and the person to whom she reported. During the meeting, Ms. Schroeder expressed her surprise at both the audit report and its findings, and subtly indicated that she would have expected to have been appraised of that situation. Mr. Lightheuser shrugged off Ms. Schroeder's concern, indicating that no organization likes to air its "dirty laundry" during an interview and indicated the problems are relatively minor. He's confident she's quite qualified to handle them.

To add insult to injury, Mr. Lightheuser next indicated that the president of Commercial Insurance, Paul Adams, has received a letter from the board of directors expressing its concern over the findings of the audit, particularly since the audit was the basis for Mr. Hickman's termination. The board has requested a quarterly report on the status of the resolution of the problems until they are all resolved.

On the bright side, as Mr. Lightheuser sees it, Mr. Adams is very excited about moving forward with their information systems. Specifically, he is interested in making major strides in the area of office automation and implementation of decision support systems for top management. Mr. Adams, in conjunction with the information systems steering committee, is fully behind these projects and would like to have them initiated as soon as possible.

Ms. Schroeder explained her concern about the level of commitment being imposed on information systems. She reminded Mr. Lightheuser that during the interview she had made a conceptual commitment to begin implementation of online systems for Commercial Insurance's major applications over the next 2 years. She said she made that commitment when she was unaware of the serious problems that the board of directors wants corrected now. Resolving the audit problems and initiating a major effort in the areas of office automation and executive-level decision support systems place an enormous and likely impossible work load on the information systems function.

Mr. Lightheuser acknowledged the exceedingly difficult challenge. He indicated that that is why Commercial was so careful to select the best possible candidate and that he, Mr. Adams, and the other members of the top management team have the utmost confidence in her ability to rise to the challenge.

As gracefully as possible, Ms. Schroeder retreated from the meeting and returned to her office to reassess the situation. After reviewing the work load implications of reworking Commercial's major systems, resolving the problems raised in the audit, and initiating advance office and decision support systems projects, Ms. Schroeder concluded that it is a totally unrealistic situation. To check her judgment, she had separate luncheons with her colleagues and "mentors" to ask them what they think of the situation. Without any prompting by Ms. Schroeder, they all concurred—it's an impossible task to proceed with all projects concurrently. She shared the situation with her immediate staff, and they became exceedingly concerned. They feel they have neither the qualifications nor the skills to move forward in the online advance office systems and decision support systems. In addition, the resources they do have are so busy maintaining the existing systems, they don't have any slack to start new projects.

Ms. Schroeder is uncertain as to how to proceed. Since Commercial just fired her predecessor, it is clear that this organization is capable of terminating someone who doesn't deliver. She at this point is not sure whether it's better to confront the situation with management and explain that their expectations are just unrealistic and risk the possibility that they will think she's not delivering. Or would it be better to make a best-effort attempt and give them as much as possible, working as hard as she can. When they see all the effort she's put into it, will they realize that she and her staff have worked as hard as they could and delivered as much as they could?

ASSIGNMENT

1. If you were Ms. Schroeder, how would you proceed?
2. Reflecting back, what could Ms. Schroeder have done during the job interview to better protect herself from the rather unwieldy situation she now faces?

Cooper Manufacturing is a medium-sized manufacturer with annual sales of $500 million per year. It is primarily a job-shop manufacturer, known for its ability in custom manufacturing projects primarily involving metal fabrication.

Over the past 20 years, Cooper has been able to automate most of its major transaction-oriented computer-based information systems with marginal success. The major complaint about the systems is that they assist primarily just in the transaction/clerical area. They provide little support for middle- and upper-level management decision making.

In an effort to improve Cooper's information systems, Cheryl Glass, vice president of information systems, recently brought in a new systems development manager, Doug Vogel, from a competitor. Mr. Vogel had a reputation for doing innovative things in the area of information systems development, and the general and top management of his previous employer were extremely pleased with the types of information systems support they had received.

Mr. Vogel had been particularly successful in implementing a heuristic development in the systems analysis design process as a way to more accurately refine end-user requirements and reduce the systems development process. He also was quite acute in selecting the best information systems development tools available and ensuring thereby that his staff was as productive as the technology would allow.

When Mr. Vogel arrived at Cooper Manufacturing, he was prepared to implement the technologies and techniques that he had been so successful with prior to joining Cooper Manufacturing. Unfortunately, he ran into a serious problem. The systems analysis and design staff had recently gone through a revamping of their systems development methodologies. They had a rather substantial systems development methodology that had evolved over the years, and in their most recent revision, they had incorporated the latest in structured techniques into their old methodology. Having been involved in its development, the staff had a strong commitment to the methodology.

In assessing the methodology, Vogel quickly decided that it was entirely too procedure- and rule-oriented and was exceptionally time consuming to use as a systems development guide. The staff also had made no provision for incorporating heuristic or prototyping techniques into their systems development methodology.

In a staff meeting, Mr. Vogel raised heuristic and prototyping concepts with the staff, but their response was immediate defensiveness. Most of them had not heard of a heuristic or prototyping technique, but felt it was a way to develop systems for sloppy designers who didn't have enough discipline to do it right. They argued that there was no way to have your cake and eat it too. They stated that if a sloppy approach to systems development, such as heuristics or prototyping, were to be used, you would have to be willing to give up the rigor and discipline of good formal procedures and good structured techniques. Overall, their general response was quite negative.

After the meeting, a couple of the younger systems analysts stuck around and indicated some interest in the concepts Mr. Vogel was proposing. They had friends working at other organizations who had been using heuristic or prototyping concepts and were quite positive about them. The younger analysts did stress the importance of having the right tools available to use such a process, but indicated that if Mr. Vogel was interested in pursuing the concept at Cooper Manufacturing, they would be interested in giving it a try. However, they expressed concern that the "old guard" might create some problems. The "old guard" might view their work as a breaking of the rules that had very carefully been developed by the leaders in the systems analysis and design group.

Mr. Vogel feels he has a tricky situation on his hands. He knows a better way to approach systems development, but he doesn't want to get cross-wise with the systems analysis and design staff, many of whom are senior to him in experience in systems development. He knows that if he tries the heuristic approach and it fails, there's going to be a lot of "I told you so." He's also concerned that if he pulls the young designers off to the side and works with the methodology, it might cause a division among the staff and some serious hard feelings that could be detrimental to the two young analysts.

ASSIGNMENT

1. What would you suggest Mr. Vogel do to try to implement the more advanced concepts for systems development?
2. Consider the types of problems that Mr. Vogel might run into with his strategy, and suggest what he should do should those difficulties arise.

In 1982, Corona Corporation did not have a good year. Sales totaled $105 million compared with $106 million in 1981. More important, net income dropped to $577,000 (31 cents per share) from $1,049,000 (57 cents per share). In its 1982 annual report, Corona Corporation stated, "Obviously management is not pleased with performance, but we know where the problems lie, and we are dealing with them."

Corona Corporation, located in Denver, Colorado, manufactures interior and industrial products. Interior products include items such as acoustic ceiling panels and modern office work stations consisting of low walls, bookcases, desks, and credenzas. Industrial products include plastic nettings and tubes, insulator pads, and hydraulic mulch. Corona employs 1450 people in manufacturing facilities located in North Carolina, Georgia, Utah, and Colorado. Company showrooms are in Denver, Chicago, and New York. Three technical centers are located in Denver and its suburbs.

Early in 1983, management acted in response to the poor 1982 business year. The broad array of commercial interior products was formed into two distinct product lines with separate objectives, marketing plans, and sales forces. The sales force was increased. The Chicago showroom was upgraded, and a new showroom in New York was unveiled. In addition, product management was reorganized to assure timely introduction of new and improved lines. The work-station product was completely revised to accommodate computers, a new wood desk with space-saving benefits was introduced, and new and expanded selections of color fabrics for ceilings and panels were developed.

Additionally, moves were made to make Corona Corporation a more efficient producer. The computer was singled out as a major contributor in this effort. Since 1980, IBM's Communications Oriented Production Information and Control System (COPICS) had been in operation in the company's largest manufacturing facility in Ogden, Utah. It was decided to adapt that package for use in two of the company's other plants. In addition, Gerry Moeller, the manager of data processing, was instructed to come up with a long-range information systems plan.

Moeller had no experience with developing an MIS plan and knew neither the format such a plan should take nor exactly what the plan should contain. With no guide to follow, Moeller, in consultation with some of his key staff members, created the plan which follows. He delivered it to Corona senior management in October 1983.

MANAGEMENT INFORMATION SYSTEMS 1984 LONG-RANGE PLAN

SITUATION ANALYSIS

Mission

The management information systems department manages the cost-effective adoption and use of information management technologies.

Functions

MIS:

Operates a "mainframe" computer system and data communication network to provide users with reliable, controlled, and timely data-processing service.

Maintains installed application systems through the use of a service request system.

New application development is achieved through the purchase of software where possible. Such systems are applied at a corporate level.

Monitors information systems technologies and company needs to suggest adoption of new systems when justified.

CURRENT RESOURCES

Summary

MIS is providing primarily transaction processing systems (i.e., A/P, billing, etc.). Data developed by these systems is summarized to provide information to middle management. MIS must find ways to apply computers to management's information needs.

Personnel

The staff has been expanded as planned during the last year, with the addition of an applications programmer and an operations support programmer. This increase allowed cross training, education, and formalization of procedures. Additional personnel and improved skills will be necessary to support the increased use of online systems.

Hardware

A larger CPU and associated controllers were installed in late 1983. An additional disk storage unit will be installed in May 1984. This equipment, with the addition of disks as required, will last through the end of 1985. A larger 4381 CPU and improved tape equipment will be required early in 1986. Our installed disks, printer, etc., will work with the 4381 CPU. Terminal equipment will be added as required.

System Software

The DOS/VSE operating system is used in conjunction with the VM/SP operating systems to provide the capacity to support batch and online processing. CICS, an IBM-program product, is used to provide our online processing environment. DL/1, another IBM product, is used to provide database management and control. COBOL and RPGII are our primary programming languages. ZEKE, an operations scheduling software package is being used to schedule and document operations.

Applications Software

Financial systems (accounts payable, accounts receivable, and general ledger) have been written in house over the years. These systems are to be replaced with purchased packages during 1985.

COPICS software is being installed to support manufacturing applications. Modules addressing the following areas are being implemented at the Ogden, High Point, and Plastic Plants.

Inventory accounting
Material requirements planning (MRP)
Sales forecasting and planning
Product costing
Order entry and shipping management
Purchasing
Production order preparation (shop order release)

As project managers and educational resources from either MIS or the user areas become available, these applications will be extended to our plants in Augusta, Pueblo, and possibly Laramie.

End-User Software

SAS, an end-user software product, was planned for 1984 but was not installed because of lack of support from proposed users. Microcomputers appear to be a preferred means of providing end-user computing.

EVALUATION

Strengths

Progress has been made in the following areas:

Education via the use of Deltak materials
Cross training in operation and CICS programming
Scheduling and operations control via ZEKE software
Project management and education support of COPICS projects
Mainstream hardware and systems software

Weaknesses

Staff has been assembled and trained assuming purchase of all major software; consequently, the department has very little systems design skills.

The small technical staff and considerable breadth of software installed makes us dependent upon a few key individuals.

New applications are achieved using purchased software. The user has been responsible for selecting the proper features and managing the installation, with assistance from MIS. In some cases, these installations have not moved as rapidly as they could have. More support of these projects from MIS is necessary.

COMPETITIVE SITUATION

Our policy of hiring at entry-level has reduced competition for staff. A good career path, adequate salary advancement, and a positive environment have reduced our risk of losing staff.

The enthusiasm with which users have adopted microcomputer spreadsheets has, in some cases, diverted them from what in our view would be better, long-term solutions.

TRENDS

Greater use of computers of all types, particularly microcomputers, is anticipated. We believe the mainframe computer will continue to be the key to transaction processing systems and will control a data communication network that will link WP, PC, and DP equipment at all locations. End-users will become more involved in query and ad hoc reporting use of the mainframe computers to provide data for their spreadsheets.

ACTION PLANS

Replace or add transaction systems to support the company's operational system needs. Systems are to use DL/1 database management system and a corporate data structure. Data developed in these systems will be available to query and/or ad hoc reporting systems.

Transaction systems will be designed, where possible, to allow later distribution of additional mainframe computers to plants while maintaining central control.

Replace current order entry system with COPICS order entry and shipping management modules. The current system has become very difficult to maintain, does not address the needs of the furniture business, and does not use DL/1, our database manager. Ogden Board and Plastics applications to be complete by the end of 1984. Furniture divisions to be converted during 1985. Remaining divisions to be converted by early 1986.

Replace current accounts payable, accounts receivable, and general ledger systems with purchased online systems (to be completed by the end of 1985). A/R is dependent on an obsolete minicomputer and programming language and does not provide a number of important features. Establishment of a centralized A/P function is being hampered by the old batch-oriented system.

Replace current standard cost calculation systems with the COPICS product cost module. This module operates online using the COPICS bills of material and component costs. Provisions for comparison between standard and actual cost and a "what if" cost calculator are provided.

Extend use of the COPICS purchasing module to all plants. Ogden Stores is using the system. Add High Point by the end of 1984. Remaining plants by early 1986. This system should reduce purchase prices through the use of a quotation file. It will also provide the receipt data as an input to the accounts payable system.

Establish corporate information network that allows data to be exchanged between WP, PC, and DP equipment at any Corona location.

In conjunction with the information resources coordinating committee (IRCC) and the information resources planning committee (IRPC) establish a 5-year data communication plan for communications between WP, PC, and DP equipment at all Corona locations. Complete by end of 1984.

Provide message exchange via COPICS CORMES message systems by late 1985.

Through the (IRCC), limit purchases of microcomputers to those that will be able to be attached to the corporate information network.

Provide a query system that will allow data developed by transaction systems to be easily extracted and manipulated or passed to a PC for further analysis. Reduce the requirement for paper sales reports.

Assure MIS capabilities are available to assist in solution of operating problems and achievement of corporate goals.

Educate user management in the use of MIS technology so they will be better able to properly use it in their organizations.

Attempt to better align MIS plans with operating group needs through more contact with user management.

Respond in a very timely way to all requests from upper management for information or analysis.

Provide additional MIS project management and systems design capabilities to assure projects are completed on time.

Add an MIS graduate to provide additional systems design and user-requirement definition skills.

Improve MIS's ability to schedule and monitor progress on those systems projects being directed by the users.

Provide necessary personnel, skills, and procedures to allow MIS to assume control of important systems projects where the user is unable or unwilling to manage the project.

Provide good to excellent day-to-day operations.

Establish formal performance measurements (uptime, reruns, project estimates, etc.).

Continue to improve documentation, procedures, and controls.

Figure 1 is a history of an MIS growth. Figure 2 shows our planned MIS expense budget for the next 4 years.

Figure 1 Expense trends

			Budget			
	1979	1980	1981	1982	1983	1984
Number of staff	16	14	17	10	10	11
Overall expense	457	545	697	563	587	778
Expense per person	29	39	41	56	59	71
Percentage increase		34	5	37	5	20

Figure 2 Four-year MIS expense plan
(Thousands of dollars)

	1984	1985	1986	1987
Personnel				
Current staff (11 people)	375	413	454	499
Systems analyst (1985)		25	28	30
Systems programmer (5/85)		12	26	29
Total personnel	375	450	507	558
Hardware				
CPU				
Current 4341 CPU	110	110		
Memory upgrade (1985)		20		
New 4381 CPU (1986)			200	200
	110	130	200	200
Disk storage				
Current (4four 3370s)	35	35	35	35
Add 3370s: 10/84 AP	2	9	9	9
2/85 AR		7	9	9
12/85			9	9
12/86				9
	37	51	62	71

	1984	1985	1986	1987
Tape drives				
Current	22	22		
Upgrade to 6250 BPI			75	75
	22	22	75	75
Printers	50	50	50	50
Communications				
Current	90	80	70	70
Additions: 1985		20	20	20
1986			15	15
1987				15
	90	100	105	120
Repairs	50	55	60	66
Total hardware	396	459	614	653
Software				
Systems				
Current	20	22	24	26
Query/ad hoc reporting	5	5	6	6
Performance measure and tune		5	8	12
Advanced communications			20	20
	25	32	58	64
Application				
Current	60	66	72	80
Additional COPICS		12	18	18
Accounts payable	17	24	23	23
Accounts receivable		20	29	27
General ledger		15	22	21
Payroll/personnel			15	22
Fixed asset				15
	77	137	179	206
Total software	102	169	237	270

Figure 2 (continued)

	1984	1985	1986	1987
User charge back (equipment)	-80	-90	-100	-110
Total MIS expense	793	987	1258	1371
Number of staff	11	13	13	13
Cost per person	72	76	97	105
Percentage increase		5	27	9

ASSIGNMENT

1. Assume that you are a consultant hired by the senior management of Corona Corporation. Write a consulting report evaluating the adequacy and format of the long-range MIS plan. Be sure to identify strengths of the plan as well as any weaknesses you discover. In addition, for the senior management, comment in your report on the following issues: (1) the policy of obtaining applications only through the purchase of software packages, (2) the policy on microcomputers expressed in the section on "Action Plans," (3) the plan to hire an MIS graduate to work on system design, and (4) the overall handling of end-user computing.

INTRODUCTION

In June 1982, it was announced that Western Retailing, Inc., would be acquired by East Products, Inc. One of the most serious problems of the combined company would be the provision of information services. The narrative that follows provides some perspective on the information systems function in both organizations.

CORPORATE MIS BACKGROUNDS

East Products

At the time the acquisition was consummated (September 1982), East Products was a $1.2 billion per year retail operation consisting primarily of 120 retail outlets whose format was based on merchandise offered in a semiannual catalog. East was highly centralized, with all operations controlled out of a small city in the Washington, D.C. area. All merchandising, buying, accounting, and data processing operations were performed at corporate headquarters. Figure

1 shows East's corporate structure at the time of the acquisition.

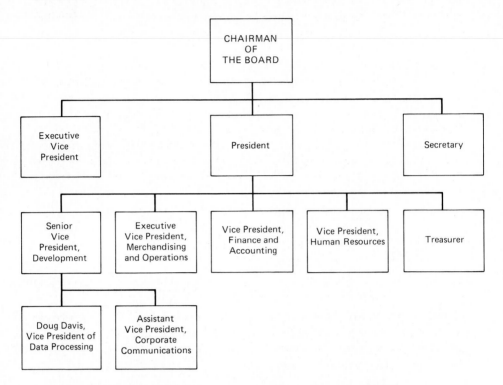

Figure 1 Organization structure of East Products.

The position of vice president of MIS was new for East, established when the incumbent, Doug Davis, was recruited to turn around the data processing department. Prior to that time, an assistant vice president had responsibility for MIS and reported to the VP of human resources. East had experienced a succession of data processing managers, each with a different approach to automating the administrative functions and installing point of sale (POS) capability in the stores. Each of these efforts, whether using distributed or centralized processing, met with very limited success. East's competition, however, was proceeding well with both POS and point of order (POO--a method of automating order taking via CRTs), which accounts for the procession of DP managers through East. This inability to match the competition became a sore spot for East's executives, especially since the industry East was involved in was controlled by a small number of individuals who had known each other for years. East therefore decided to upgrade the position of head of MIS, allowing the VP to report directly to top management.

After a long search, Doug Davis was recruited from a major manufacturer. Mr. Davis inherited a potpourri of hardware and software, the remnants of his predecessors. He brought a core of MIS professionals with him from his old firm, re-organized the department (see Figure 2), and began planning to move East into a new generation of hardware and software that he hoped would bring East not even with the competition, but leap-frog beyond what competitors had developed.

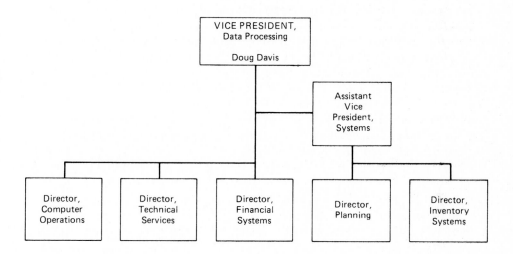

Figure 2 East Products data processing organization.

The heart of the East systems was based on Honeywell mainframes. POS registers consisted of multiple generations of NCR and DTS terminals. Some stores still had Honeywell level 6 minicomputers, the vestiges of an aborted attempt to distribute processing to the stores. Despite the large investment in hardware, software, and staff, East was not getting a return on the money it had invested in MIS. The

POS systems and the systems they fed were not responsive. It was not unusual for buyers at corporate headquarters to experience data lags of up to 20 days. This means that it could be 20 days after an item was sold before a buyer knew the item had to be replenished. This was especially critical during the Christmas season, when East did the majority of its business. The accounting department experienced similar delays, with monthly closing occurring 40 to 45 days after actual month end.

East's systems had been designed and built when East was a small, regional company. The frustrated DP staff continued to maintain the systems even though East had grown 10-fold and was now a national leader in its industry. The frustration level of the users, however, had resulted in user departments developing their own DP structures, using retrieval languages and analysis in their own areas to meet DP needs. Personal computers abounded as soon as they came on the market. Each department developed the ability to produce "computer generated" reports, with each department's reports showing them to be exactly on target and on budget, but with no central database to verify those reports. The distribution department went to a minicomputer, a DEC, and developed its own systems independent of the MIS department. It was into this mess that Mr. Davis stepped. He determined that a complete overhaul, with no gradual transition or conversion, was the best answer.

With the help of a nationally recognized planning firm, Mr. Davis was able to develop a multimillion dollar plan to move to an IBM-compatible, state-of-the-art environment. East's proximity to Washington, D.C., made it difficult to attract and keep MIS professionals, but the feeling was that it would be easier with IBM or IBM-type machines in the shop. Mr. Davis was from a very technical background and felt that the technology available from an IBM environment would also be the only feasible way to move the company forward. The plan was a 5-year plan. Neither the cost nor the long lead time stopped East's executive committee from endorsing the plan, since the company recognized its dire need for more timely and accurate information. At the time of the acquisition, East was 1 year into the plan. A POO/POS system had been developed on Amdahl mainframes, utilizing IBM's database (IMS) and the database telecommunications monitor, IMS-DC. A limited number of stores (16) were to experience their first Christmas season on the new system in December 1982. Vendor problems, learning curves, and lack of strong user involvement were causing response, reliability, and user problems with the system. MIS was physically located in very cramped quarters in some warehouse facilities, causing some morale problems. Part of the staff was working on new systems in the IBM/Amdahl environment, while others were stuck working on the Kludge systems on the Honeywell mainframe. The rapid changes in the East MIS department were taking their toll even without the complications of adding other data processing departments.

While all this was happening and prior to the Western acquisition, another small retailer, running an operation of 17 stores, was added to the East system. This retailer was in financial trouble and, using the "old boy" network in place in the industry, called on the management of East to buy it out. The small chain had had a functioning POO/POS system in place for years, running on DEC minicomputers. When East took over, it decided to leave the POO/POS portion of the system in place, but to transfer all buying decisions and back-office functions to East's corporate headquarters. A small part of the acquired company's DP staff was left in place to run the POO/POS system, with tapes going to East for inclusion in the administrative systems. The acquisition was a bail-out, with East personnel having little respect for methods or personnel in the small chain. The attitude of the East DP employees was that their counterparts had to be inferior since the company was not as successful as East. Further, they neither had nor were moving to state-of-the-art DP technology. A mental set for acquired companies was established, and this mental set was to affect the later acquisition of Western Retailing.

Mr. Davis's management style was very typical of data processing managers. He felt that his job, and that of his department, was to serve as a support arm to the merchandising area. He contended that MIS should listen to needs, then develop DP solutions to the company's problems. He was very much a "controller" type of manager, shouldering all blame when anything went wrong and demanding unswerving loyalty from his staff. The personnel he brought with him from his former employer all displayed this unquestioning loyalty. There was some friction in the department caused by bringing in managers with no retail experience to manage

East employees who had many years' service. Mr. Davis recognized this problem, but felt there was no alternative since the existing staff had failed to solve the problems in the past and had no experience with the new technology. Because there had not been sufficient time when the acquisition took place to develop major deliverables according to the 5-year plan, Mr. Davis had not been able to establish credibility for himself or his department with the user community. The users and management were expecting the credibility to come with the new systems to be developed.

Western Retailing

Western was a retailing organization with, for the most part, the same type of business as East Products. Western was on track for an $800 million plus year when the June announcement was made. While East had grown by building new stores (except for the acquisition of the small chain just prior to the Western transaction), Western had grown by a combination of building new stores plus a number of acquisitions. For the most part, Western's acquisitions were of very small, two- to four-store chains, that had no automation at all. One exception to this was the acquisition of a chain of 11 midwestern stores that were supported very well by a POS and administrative system based on an NCR mainframe. Each of Western's acquisitions was allowed to run fairly autonomously, so conflict between those acquired and Western was held to a minimum. There was considerable doubt as to the wisdom of this strategy, but it had not been tested as yet. Western was therefore very deccentralized. Merchandising, buying, and accounting functions were performed regionally, with each region being treated as a subsidiary.

Data processing, however, was largely centralized. A DP staff at Western's headquarters in Wisconsin supported most MIS needs. There were two kinds of store systems supported, depending on store format. A POO/POS system supported three regions, while two other larger regions were supported on POS systems only (their stores did not support POO functions). Three smaller regions had manual store and administrative systems, with all accounting functions automated at the central site. The POO/POS system was based on DEC minicomputers, and was strongly supported by users, management, and MIS. The accounting and administrative systems were batch systems, supported on an IBM mainframe. The back-office functions were, in 1980-1981, less than optimal.

MIS at Western suffered the same lack of stature as the East MIS department, with a director of DP reporting to the vice president of administration. The VP of administration, recognizing his shortcomings in attempting to manage the MIS function, recommended that a VP of MIS be recruited to clean up the systems area. The recommendation was accepted, and Jack Wilson was recruited from a large Chicago conglomerate. Mr. Wilson quickly stopped a plan to distribute processing to stores, and concentrated MIS efforts in building a business-oriented staff who could attack the financial, merchandising, and administrative needs of the company.

Extensive recruiting for this "type" of MIS professional resulted in the MIS department structure shown in Figure 3. The basic systems were stabilized in 1981, and MIS shifted its emphasis to an information center implementation, user-direct systems, and planning for an environment in which future systems would be of the decision support or management information systems type versus data processing or clerical automation systems. There was a conscious effort to develop an elitism on the part of the staff. Mr. Wilson

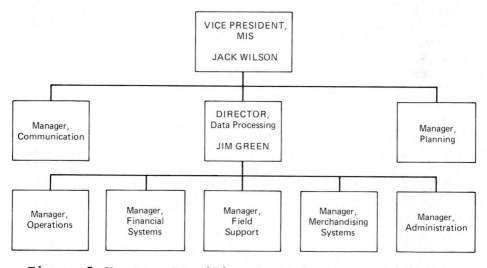

Figure 3 Western Retailing data processing organization.

attempted to stretch each of the managers, often working directly with the managers and bypassing their directors. The department became associated with an MIS research center at a local state university in an attempt to foster a broader perspective for MIS and to provide enrichment for the staff. Mr. Wilson was a student of IBM management principles and frequently referred to current articles on MIS management to find solutions to situations he faced. It was said that on occasion he practiced "management by conflict" to force managers out of traditional methods of attacking DP problems.

Jack Wilson considered himself, and was recognized by other executives in the company, to be a businessperson first and an MIS professional second. As such, he was heavily involved in business decisions and was eventually given control of a critical merchandising program, a large departure from the traditional VP of MIS duties. This was far different from the role chosen for the head of MIS by Doug Davis of East. The managers Jack Wilson attracted to his organization considered Mr. Wilson to be the prototype of an MIS professional of tomorrow—the "chief information officer" often referred to in *HBR* articles. As a result of Mr. Wilson's leadership, MIS enjoyed a high degree of credibility within the Western organization, even though MIS personnel recognized that there were stages of Nolan's development yet to be reached.

STAGES OF THE ACQUISITION

Phase 1

The first phase of the acquisition, at least as far as MIS was concerned, began in June 1982. The announcement of the impending takeover came as a complete shock to the MIS department. Emotions ran high, primarily because no one other than Western's chairman of the board had any details. It would be revealed later that there were no details, but the business-oriented staff at Western felt that a merger or acquisition of such magnitude (a move resulting in a $2 billion company) would have been carefully planned. When some of the details did become known, it was revealed that other than the president/CEO of Western, no one else would be affected. It was publicly announced that Western, which was experiencing a rapid recovery from a decline that had eroded profits for a 2-year period, would be left alone as a wholly owned subsidiary.

Although some news articles suggested otherwise, most of the staff was satisfied that the progress the MIS department had enjoyed would continue, since Western would be allowed to pursue its own destiny. No contact was offered from either MIS department other than one or two meetings between the two vice presidents. The lack of any official contact resulted in the staff's opinions being based on rumors and common vendor contacts. The Western staff, however, felt the East DP group was wrong to attempt an IMS DB/DC POO/POS system and a complete redesign. Meanwhile, the East MIS department felt Western was not state-of-the-art because Western used an old minicomputer system to support POD/POS and did not have a formal DBMS. The Western also got the reputation of a university think-tank environment that thought about problems and the future, but did nothing about them.

The Western staff's elitism grew even more pronounced when Western started to hear rumors of East's data lag problem and the amount being expended to move to the new generation of systems. The Western system allowed buyers to know immediately what the in-stock position was, and reports showed inventory as of the prior day. Financial systems closed within 10 days of month-end, and could be accelerated to 1 week if manual procedures were to be streamlined. Each of these factors contributed to the smug feelings of the Western DP group.

Phase 2

Phase 2 of the acquisition began on December 22, 1982. One by one, the Western executives were called to a meeting where they learned that East had decided to merge Western into the new stores division of East Products. All executives (vice president and above) were offered positions at East's corporate headquarters or a severance package. MIS was now affected directly by the acquisition. Jack Wilson, Western's VP of MIS, was being transferred to East's headquarters as corporate VP of planning, reporting to a senior corporate VP. Jim Green, Western's director of DP, was told he would be reporting directly to Doug Davis. The stories of the mess in East's MIS department hit home at Western as the staff realized that they now reported into that organization. At this point, none of the managers had even met Doug Davis.

This phase lasted until well into January, with no contact of any kind between the two departments. Turnover began to hit the Western staff as people were lost from every area. People who had been recruited into a particular environment began to see that environment change, and many sought employment elsewhere. The staff was especially put on edge by 2-inch headlines in the morning newspaper declaring "150 Jobs Wiped Out at Western Retailing." The article went on to state that redundant functions, including accounting and data processing, would be consolidated at East's corporate headquarters. The paper was quoting Western's former chairman of the board; he denied the comments and demanded a retraction from the paper. A note of clarification buried in the next day's paper did nothing to quiet the storm of controversy that followed the first article.

Phase 3

Phase 3 of the acquisition was occasioned by a visit from Doug Davis to Western's headquarters. A schedule was developed to allow each of the key managers at Western to meet with Mr. Davis for a 1-hour session. This was the first time most of these people had even seen Mr. Davis. The meetings were set for February 2, 1983. Mr. Davis had met with his key managers to develop a list of concerns/questions (see Figure 4). The list shows that as soon as the decision was announced at East's headquarters, the assumption was the Western way of doing business, including the MIS department, was going to be dropped in favor of East's procedures. This attitude was picked up by each of the managers when speaking with Mr. Davis. The meetings were very strained, with Mr. Davis starting the interviews asking whether the managers were willing to relocate. The next day, most of the managers met with recruiters to begin a job search. The tension felt by the managers was picked up by the rank-and-file data processing employees, and turnover started to decimate the staff.

Figure 4 Concerns and issues involved in data processing with the acquisition of Western Retailing by East Products.

Can our existing hardware and applications handle the additional work loads?

  Can the detail file and databases grow enough?

  What additional disks and tape drives, memory, etc., will we need?

  Even with additional printers, can we process and print reports in a timely fashion?

  What will data lag be?

How will Western's way of doing business change?

What kind of timeframes, if any, does corporate management have in mind for the integration?

Relative to the integration, is there a higher priority on some functions than on others (i.e., payroll, A/P, inventory, etc.)?

Will the initial integration include all of Western's subs?

The Western integration committee should be organized as quickly as possible. It should either have multiple levels or originally consist of those people who will be directly responsible for doing the work (i.e., manager level).

How does this change the 4-year strategic plan?

  What assumptions are we making in new systems that are no longer true?

  What additional areas should new systems investigate?

  Does this change the POO implementation strategy?

  What additional staffing and contract services do we need?

  How will Western's different store types affect where we are headed?

  What is the impact on existing planned and active projects—does this take priority?

We need to launch a fact-finding mission aimed at determining how Western operates and how DP supports it (i.e., the "stake" in the ground).

  What is its merchandise mix? How compatible is it with ours?

  How decentralized is it?

  How does it handle credit cards, credit vouchers, gift certificates, layaways, etc.?

  What type of cash controls does it have?

What type of system backup facilities exist?

Does it have a receivables system?

What areas of the company does Western DP support that East DP does not (i.e., voice communications)?

Is one of the long-range goals complete integration of its organization and functions?

Do we need a full-time person from East's data processing to be at Western during the transition period?

Would it be beneficial to move some East DP personnel to Western DP as soon as possible to assist in the transition?

Would we be better off to leave the two companies separate for the next 12 to 16 months, with several interim objectives aimed at making us more compatible at the end of that time frame?

Can a bridge be built from their system to ours?

If the item-matching process is to take place again, it should be completely accomplished very early in the integration process.

Will there be inventory reduction sales to reduce levels of noncommon merchandise?

If there will be only partial DP integration, such as with our last transition, more controls should be designed in up front.

If all buying will be done here, how soon should that begin?

What additional reporting must be done for financial and management purposes (LIFO additions, etc.)?

Will Western convert to our chart of accounts?

Will Western mirror all our procedures in the field (such as our last acquisition did)?

Identify and secure key technical, operational, systems, and management personnel; that is, offer incentives to stay.

Concerns for Doug Davis

The DP person appointed to manage the integration should not have any other responsibilities for the duration of the activity.

What should happen to Western's DP efforts which are currently under development; should they be frozen?

What are the components of the Western DP budget? Is it approved?

In an effort to bring the two data processing staffs face to face and eliminate the distrust and rumors, a "cultural exchange" meeting was set up at East's headquarters for key staff members to formally present themselves to each other. The meeting was delayed repeatedly and was finally set for March.   Once again, communications between the two staffs ceased, awaiting the meeting.   The presentations were made, but many of the suspicions remained since the corporate cultures were very different.   Also, by this time, most of the Western staff had made their decision to leave and really had no interest in any exchange with the DP staff of East.

The Western staff returned to Wisconsin with a list of responsibilities assigned by Mr. Davis to work on for integrating the staffs.   The Western staff felt that they were being asked to compromise on everything they had built over the preceding 2 years.   Both staffs suffered heavily from the "NIH" (not invented here) syndrome.   The East MIS staff felt it was only a matter of time before their systems replaced the inferior systems and procedures of Western. The Western staff was beginning to feel their days were indeed numbered.   The job searches initiated after the meeting with Mr. Davis began to bear fruit, and Western lost five of the top MIS staff to other companies.

ASSIGNMENT

1. Write a consulting report stating what should be done <u>at this time</u> to solve the problems in data processing caused by the corporate acquisition.
2. How, if you could go back to the time the acquisition occurred, would you have avoided the present data processing problems?

INTRODUCTION

Eastern International Hotels, Inc., is an aggressive and fast-growing hotel chain headquartered in Boston, Massachusetts. Eastern was founded in 1947 when a group of investors bought a small New England hotel chain and began building new hotels in major American cities. Today, Eastern has approximately 160 hotels in the continental United States. In 1974, Eastern became a wholly owned subsidiary of International Finance Corporation. Compared with such popular hotel chains as Holiday Inn, Sheraton, and Hilton, Eastern is still a small- to medium-sized company, but management is pleased with its profitability and growth, and plans are underway to build more hotels.

Figures 1 and 2 show the organizational structure of Eastern's corporate management and the upper levels of the management information systems department. Besides the individuals listed in Figure 2, the MIS department also employs:

6 systems managers, functionally organized by user departments
5 systems programmers
5 operators and data entry personnel

4 financial and operations research analysts
11 senior analysts
8 analyst/programmers
2 associate analysts
7 programmers

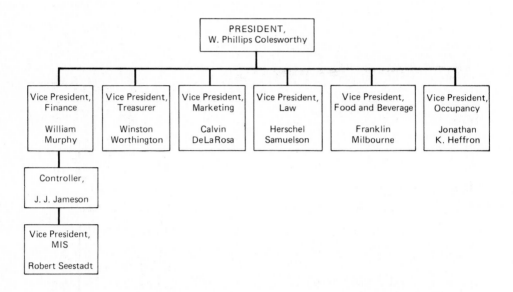

Figure 1   Eastern International Hotels: Corporate management.

Eastern International Hotels pioneered computerized hotel reservations in 1967 with a centrally located online reservation system. Currently, all of Eastern's computing facilities, including roughly 130 online terminals (CRTs) for reservation purposes, are located in Boston. Reservations for all Eastern hotels throughout the country are handled by toll-free calls to the terminal operators in Boston.

In 1974, Eastern signed a contractual agreement with Easy-Lodge Motels, Inc., to allow Easy-Lodge to utilize Eastern's excess computing capacity for an online reservation system similar to Eastern's. The Easy-Lodge Corporation currently owns 218 motels nationwide, and the contract is binding until 1987. Easy-Lodge uses approximately 90 of their own terminals, which are tied directly to Eastern's computers, for reservations. In 1984, Eastern will have recovered all systems development costs, and the Easy-Lodge contract will begin contributing primarily profits.

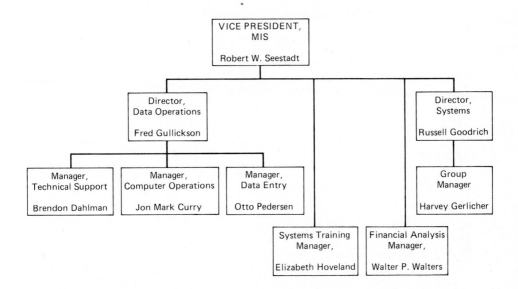

Figure 2 Eastern International Hotels: Department of Management Information Systems.

As might be expected, Eastern and Easy-Lodge do a seasonal business. In terms of online reservations activity, there are noticeable peaks each year during March and August, the August peak being the largest. Historically, an accepted rule of thumb is that, because of normal business growth, next year's March peak will be roughly equivalent to this year's August peak. Despite differing growth patterns at Eastern and Easy-Lodge, their combined reservations activity has followed this pattern for the first few years of the Easy-Lodge contract.

In February 1976, Eastern purchased an IBM 370/158 to replace Honeywell equipment. The 370 was expected to be adequate to handle projected applications growth for 3 years. However, a change in the reservations system software led to an increase in CPU utilization per reservation. This development, on top of an underestimated growth forecast, resulted in a much higher rate of growth in CPU activity than was expected in 1977.

During the March 1977 peak, the 370 CPU was running at 95 percent capacity, with the result that batch throughput was virtually nonexistent. Batch test jobs were taking 3 to 5 days to complete. It was clear that the 370 would not be able to handle the August 1977 peak, and plans were made in April 1977 to lease another 370/158 for the 2-year interim prior to the installation of the next generation of IBM hardware (3033), which was expected to be available in 1979. The second 370 arrived in May and was operational in June 1977.

CURRENT OPERATIONS

CPU utilization at Eastern, as with most large organizations, is made up of online processing and batch processing. At Eastern, the demand for CPU cycles comes largely from online transactions, and this demand is consistently most heavy during the day shift. The online activity on both systems is maintained by a CICS package which controls the internal communications and scheduling of the online terminals.

Batch processing consists of test jobs and regularly scheduled production activity. Batch test jobs are normally run during the day and are a very small percentage of daytime CPU utilization. Batch production jobs are run between 1 A.M. and 5 A.M., when online activity is at a minimum.

CPU capacity problems are therefore the result of online processing. When daytime CPU utilization reaches capacity (as was the case in March 1977), batch test jobs take an unacceptable amount of time to complete. In extreme cases, online transactions backlog internally and may spill over into the second and third shifts, making it difficult to complete batch production work in the early morning hours.

Although batch processing in the first half of 1977 is up 19 percent from the same period the year before, the majority of batch processing on both CPUs is done during the third shift, making batch processing a minor consideration when discussing Eastern's CPU utilization.

The following online applications are, for the most part, responsible for Eastern's data processing activity:

System A (370/158)	System B (370/158)
Eastern reservation system Easy-Lodge reservation system	Input processing Open receivables Leasing system General file Accounts payable Unit history

Occupancy at Eastern is divided into two categories—short-term rental and long-term leasing. Rentals are the vast majority of Eastern's business, and room rentals are handled through the reservations software (system A). There are, however, those individuals whose accommodations at Eastern are their primary place of residence. For these customers, Eastern offers a 6-month leasing arrangement at lower rates. Leasing transactions are handled through the leasing system (system B). Although leasing accounts for a very small percentage of Eastern's revenue, its corporate policy is to accommodate all types of customers, and management is grateful for the steady occupancy that leasing provides. Unlike Eastern, all the Easy-Lodge business is booked through its reservation system.

Most of the other applications on system B involve standard accounting programs and files. A reservation at Eastern requires two separate activities. The terminal operator first enters the reservation into the Eastern reservation system. This is followed by a rental agreement, which is simply an input to the open receivables system. Since many of Eastern's occupants are steady customers, such as business travelers, the rental agreement often involves little more than an update to the receivables file. Thus, for an average reservation at Eastern, system A absorbs the bulk of the internal processing.

The input processing application runs in conjunction with open receivables and accounts payable to feed input data into these systems and extract and organize appropriate information or managerial summary reports. The nature of the business therefore requires that receivables be an on-line activity, and since the open receivables and accounts payable applications are tied together throughout input processing, it is also necessary to enter payables information online. However, the output from these files, in terms of invoices, checks, and reports, is generated during regular batch production work on the third shift. Unit history is simply a history of yearly occupancy data for each of Eastern's hotels. Easy-lodge handles all its own accounting, making no use of system B.

Equipment

Figure 3 lists the data processing equipment owned and leased by Eastern International Hotels as of fall of 1977.

Figure 3 Eastern International Hotels: Data processing equipment inventory

Number	Item
2	370/158 MOD 3 (2 megabytes each)
3	1403 printers
3	2821 printer control units
1	1442 card reader
2	2914 switch units
2	3213 hard-copy consoles
6	3330 disk drives
2	3350 A2 disk drives
8	3350 B2 disk drives
1	3830 disk controller
2	3803 tape controllers
12	3420 tape drives
1	Memorex communications control unit
1	4200 datagraphix fiche unit
9	Harris channel interface units
33	Harris processors (CRT control units)
4	CRTs for remote consoles
258	CRTs for user departments
1	Datacard embossing unit
1	Sycor minicomputer and tape drive

PREPARATION FOR HARDWARE PLANNING MEETING

Robert Seestadt, vice president of MIS, scheduled a hardware planning meeting on October 10, 1977 to determine if the present computing facilities at Eastern would be adequate to meet its data processing needs for the next 2 years. Those asked to attend the meeting were Messrs. Curry, Gullickson, Dahlman, Goodrich, Gerlicher, and Walters, as well as three representatives from IBM. Mr. Walters was asked by Mr. Seestadt to prepare a 2-year forecast of projected CPU utilization. In a memo to Mr. Walters, Mr. Seestadt noted that the underestimated forecast of usage that accompanied the purchase of the original 370/158 was extremely embarrassing to the MIS department. He suggested in the memo that the unforeseen increase in utilization in 1977 was only partially caused by the change in the reservations software.

Mr. Walters asked one of his department's operations research analysts, Kathy Robinson, to prepare this for the October 10 meeting. To provide stimulation to do an outstanding job, Walters had her present results at the meeting.

After studying the problem for a few days, Ms. Robinson has gathered several items of background information:

1. A meeting with Mr. De La Rosa and one of his assistants confirmed Mr. Seestadt's suspicions that business, in terms of units rented or leased, had been growing faster than expected in 1977. The accelerated growth rate is attributed to Eastern's first national advertising campaign which occurred during the latter half of 1976, and there is a widespread optimism among corporate management that this growth rate will continue into the 1980s.

2. Mr. Curry of operations informed Ms. Robinson that during the March 1977 peak when the single 370/158 was running at near total capacity, the system was processing 5.6 million transactions per month. Based on this experience, the operations staff has concluded that, with Eastern's current applications mix, a typical IBM 370/158 is capable of handling 5 to 5.5 million transactions per month without a serious backlog of online activity. Mr. Curry explained that a transaction was simply a measurable unit of CPU activity for a given application, such as an I/O operation or an update to a data field, and

therefore not the equivalent of a business transaction. Although the different types of transactions may vary slightly in the amount of CP time required to complete the transaction, they are generally close enough to allow the number of transactions to be used as a measure of CPU activity per application. The advantage of using this type of measurement, as opposed to standard measures such as CPU cycles, was that Eastern had been measuring CPU transactions since 1975, and this type of measurement was consistent across various types of hardware and software. This, said Mr. Curry, allowed Eastern to measure computer utilization per application over a long period of time.

3. A history of CPU transactions per month per application for the period from January 1975 to August 1977 was provided by the operations department from the computer performance history file (see Figure 4). CICS transactions are available only for total data processing, and may be allocated to system A and system B based on the percentage of transactions performed by each system.

4. A partial summary of the transaction history data was prepared for Ms. Robinson by operations to compare January–September 1977 with the same period in 1976 (see Figure 5).

5. Operations also provided a graph that had been prepared on July 12, 1977 to show system A CPU utilization over a 24-hour period (see Figure 6). System B was not analyzed in this manner since it does not present the capacity problem found on system A. The data in Figure 6 prompted Ms. Robinson to ask operations if any historical information was available to show the growth in CPU utilization for different times during the day. She reasoned that the transactions per month information might, on the average, indicate excess CPU capacity, but this would be a meaningless conclusion if the system could not survive the daily peak processing periods. The only data available was a CICS performance analysis that measured the percentage of CPU utilization for a 2-hour period from 12 P.M. to 2 P.M. Ms. Robinson was informed that, beginning in May 1976, a test of this type was run once a month (see Figure 7). The right-hand column in Figure 7 shows the percentage of CPU utilization for a 10-minute peak period during the 2-hour sample.

Figure 4 Eastern International Hotels: Computer history performance

Eastern reservations		Easy-Lodge reservations		Leasing system		Unit history	
Date	Transactions	Date	Transactions	Date	Transactions	Date	Transactions
7501	806000	7501	377000	7501	23726	7501	93457
7502	791000	7502	532000	7502	20011	7502	84311
7503	845000	7503	739000	7503	19280	7503	78075
7504	850000	7504	558000	7504	18581	7504	97926
7505	855000	7505	705000	7505	17003	7505	91209
7506	880000	7506	1034000	7506	18254	7506	76135
7507	925000	7507	1378000	7507	20686	7507	73007
7508	911000	7508	1478000	7508	17945	7508	71744
7509	960000	7509	641000	7509	18797	7509	69171
7510	1083000	7510	770000	7510	17340	7510	81246
7511	1033000	7511	522000	7511	16953	7511	70336
7512	998000	7512	672000	7512	16923	7512	86326
7601	1145000	7601	699000	7601	17960	7601	95082
7602	1124000	7602	910000	7602	15908	7602	92379
7603	1286000	7603	1086000	7603	18479	7603	116004
7604	1238000	7604	1039000	7604	15492	7604	107817
7605	1230000	7605	997000	7605	13851	7605	87022
7606	1340000	7606	1294000	7606	16274	7606	85104
7607	1290000	7607	1372000	7607	14238	7607	88219
7608	1433000	7608	1372000	7608	16461	7608	95066
7609	1368000	7609	740000	7609	14073	7609	88701
7610	1432000	7610	784000	7610	14211	7610	89891
7611	1490000	7611	609000	7611	13420	7611	94255
7612	1281000	7612	595000	7612	15486	7612	81543
7701	1543000	7701	687000	7701	17397	7701	127263
7702	1513000	7702	1056000	7702	13803	7702	113083
7703	2141000	7703	1275000	7703	15241	7703	142257
7704	2099000	7704	1221000	7704	12976	7704	142257
7705	2075483	7705	1534000	7705	13305	7705	112351
7706	2131618	7706	1905000	7706	11427	7706	107278
7707	2133353	7707	2390000	7707	11526	7707	111397
7708	2482323	7708	2682000	7708	13161	7708	149116

| Input processing | | Open receivables | | Accounts payable* | |
Date	Transactions	Date	Transactions	Date	Transactions
7501	566210	7501	286764	7503	23241
7502	580636	7502	252371	7504	28198
7503	670958	7503	262038	7505	26434
7504	761485	7504	274705	7506	28927
7505	694123	7505	261471	7507	31927
7506	761210	7506	278150	7508	27825
7507	742857	7507	270423	7509	30046
7508	770464	7508	245381	7510	37196
7509	734399	7509	236561	7511	29620
7510	778741	7510	310411	7512	29281
7511	781746	7511	265075	7601	29957
7512	770591	7512	255231	7602	31475
7601	699062	7601	283954	7603	38748
7602	738684	7602	260254	7604	30432
7603	972032	7603	375199	7605	26336
7604	887579	7604	319863	7606	29552
7605	883957	7605	160218	7607	26576
7606	999232	7606	322645	7608	28397
7607	1007907	7607	279678	7609	30343
7608	952911	7608	351448	7610	28944
7609	957775	7609	338799	7611	27169
7610	981179	7610	330489	7612	30093
7611	996970	7611	371015	7701	36329
7612	907919	7612	352897	7702	31486
7701	806954	7701	420397	7703	44265
7702	871595	7702	381000	7704	38410
7703	1084691	7703	501094	7705	37045
7704	1018390	7704	415049	7706	37930
7705	965519	7705	380429	7707	34250
7706	1297186	7706	397265	7708	41941
7707	1178055	7707	347875		
7708	1544725	7708	475249		

*7501 and 7502 not available

General file		CICS control		Total transactions	
Date	Transactions	Date	Transactions	Date	Transactions
7501	119699	7501	122255	7501	2396000
7502	119058	7502	134906	7502	2515000
7503	124246	7503	149509	7503	2904000
7504	122818	7504	145325	7504	2859000
7505	111197	7505	137500	7505	2899000
7506	108665	7506	149003	7506	3334000
7507	130749	7507	357000	7507	4061000
7508	155795	7508	170709	7508	3824000
7509	172845	7509	146882	7509	3010000
7510	153156	7510	131399	7510	3362000
7511	160705	7511	106781	7511	2987000
7512	134610	7512	121621	7512	3085000
7601	129435	7601	119276	7601	3216000
7602	141176	7602	119334	7602	3457000
7603	146340	7603	137663	7603	4177000
7604	136902	7604	140497	7604	3917000
7605	117023	7605	134417	7605	3750000
7606	162662	7606	161432	7606	4415000
7607	174984	7607	136683	7607	4390000
7608	183679	7608	154073	7608	4587000
7609	149959	7609	151617	7609	3839000
7610	149143	7610	153497	7610	3936000
7611	142802	7611	171986	7611	3917000
7612	135444	7612	157000	7612	3557000
7701	154141	7701	217886	7701	4011000
7702	155791	7702	204676	7702	4343000
7703	168700	7703	276211	7703	5689000
7704	136756	7704	310194	7704	5434000
7705	151882	7705	364493	7705	5680000
7706	171876	7706	409933	7706	6531000
7707	158997	7707	441333	7707	6852000
7708	191447	7708	565192	7708	8134000

Figure 5 Eastern International Hotels: CPU transaction analysis

Application system	January–September 1976	January–September 1977	Difference	Percentage change
Leasing	142,736	120,787	-21,949	-15.38
CICS control	1,254,992.	3,224,997	1,970,005	156.97
General file	1,342,160	1,493,912	151,752	11.31
Easy-Lodge reservations	9,509,000	14,322,000	4,813,000	50.62
Input processing	8,099,139	10,020,589	1,921,450	23.72
Open receivables	2,792,058	3,703,186	911,128	32.63
Eastern reservations	11,458,000	18,392,763	6,934,763	60.50
Unit history	855,394	1,133,420	278,026	32.50
Accounts payable	271,816	339,130	67,314	24.80
Total	35,725,295	52,750,784	17,025,489	47.65

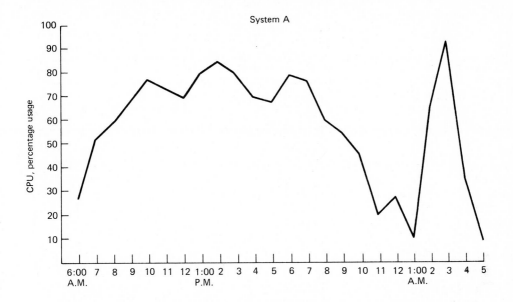

Figure 6 Eastern International Hotels: 24-hour CPU utilization.

6. Corporate management is looking seriously at the possibility of entering into a contract with the Taco Bell motel chain, offering them the same online reservation capability that Eastern currently provides to Easy-Lodge motels. If such an agreement were to be signed, it would become effective May 1, 1978. The forecast is that the transaction volume of the Taco Bell reservation system would be roughly one-half that of the Easy-Lodge system. Since Easy-Lodge and Taco Bell were unwilling to make their future business growth projections available to Eastern's management, Ms. Robinson was forced to make her estimates of their transactions growth from the Easy-Lodge growth pattern of the last $2\frac{1}{2}$ years. She felt that it would be in Eastern's best interests to develop a very optimistic forecast of transaction growth for Easy-Lodge and Taco Bell in order to be on the safe side.

Figure 7 Eastern International Hotels: CICS performance analysis.

Date	Sample time	Peak CPU performance percentage
5/10/76	1:57:58	70.9
6/7/76	1:57:20	73.5
7/12/76	1:56:24	78.0
8/9/76	1:58:28	76.2
9/13/76	1:54:16	79.2
10/11/76	1:56:10	73.9
11/8/76	1:56:18	76.4
12/13/76	1:55:02	75.1
1/10/77	1:56:32	80.5
2/7/77	1:58:26	87.9
3/14/77	1:48:53	97.2
4/11/77	1:48:03	88.0
5/9/77	1:53:21	90.1
6/7/77	1:53:31	89.8
7/11/77		
System A	1:53:19	79.3
System B	2:01:56	38.1
8/8/77		
System A	1:52:32	88.4
System B	2:02:21	42.4

7. During a second meeting with Mr. Curry to discuss the applications mix, Ms. Robinson was informed that none of the eight applications on systems A and B could be split across the two systems. The problems that would result from splitting an application would be intolerable; the increased software overhead and duplication of files would serve only to decrease available CPU capacity. Furthermore, Mr. Curry stated that in order to maintain a reasonable degree of operating efficiency, the input processing, open receivables, and accounts payable applications should be run together on the same CPU. For the same reason, if Eastern were to sign a contract with Taco Bell, the Easy-Lodge and Taco Bell applications should be run on the same machine. If Eastern rearranged its applications mix, it would have to treat each of the

following (individual applications or sets of applications) as a separate unit of software, to be run on one
system or the other:

a. Eastern reservations
b. Easy-Lodge reservations
   Taco Bell reservations
c. Input processing
   Open receivables
   Accounts payable
d. Leasing
e. Unit history
f. General file

8. The regularly scheduled batch processing activities are
   fairly evenly divided between systems A and B. In other
   words, CPU utilization between 1 A.M. and 5 A.M. is
   almost identical for both systems. Test jobs and other
   minor daytime batch work have been run entirely on system
   B since June 1977, but are, on the average, only 10-20
   percent of its daytime processing load.

ASSIGNMENT

1. Prepare Ms. Robinson's report for the October 10 hardware
planning meeting. Mr. Seestadt wants to know if the two
370/158 machines are sufficient to handle transactions
growth through 1979, particularly since the Taco Bell arrangement appears imminent. You may assume that peripherals
are not a problem, as more I/O and storage devices may be
added if necessary.

Your report should include a discussion of the problem,
any assumptions that you made and problems you encountered,
the methods and procedures that you used to analyze the
problem, your conclusions, and any supporting graphs and
charts that you feel would help in your presentation.

On Monday, October 10, 1977, a hardware capacity analysis meeting was held at the corporate headquarters of Eastern International Hotels. The focus of the meeting was a report prepared by Ms. Kathy Robinson, an operations research analyst from the MIS department. Following the formal presentation by Ms. Robinson, which dealt with known computer hardware capacity and forecasts of work load, there was a lively discussion. The meeting concluded with a consensus that current hardware (two IBM model 370/158s) could survive (perhaps barely) the March 1978 peak in transactions volume, but that steps would have to be taken to increase capacity to handle the August 1978 peak. If there was one thing all could agree on, it was that the reservation systems running on one of the 158s would be well in excess of capacity by August.

Fred Gullickson, the director of data operations was put in charge of a team to generate solutions to the CPU capacity problem. Members of the team would be Kathy Robinson, because of her now great familiarity with the problem, and Said Motamed, who would represent the technical support group and had a wealth of detailed technical knowledge. Alternatives were to be presented to Mr. Seestadt, VP of MIS on October 19, 1977. As one last charge to the team, Mr. Seestadt suggested that they look particularly hard at alternatives that might expand capacity by March 1978, thus reducing the risk that the present system might not, as hoped, handle the March business peak.

A MAJOR NEW CONSIDERATION

On October 17, 1977, Mr. Seestadt was summoned to a meeting with the senior EIH executives. At this meeting, Mr. See-stadt learned that Eastern Hotels, having outgrown its cor-porate headquarters and contemplated the construction of a new headquarters office building since 1976, had contracted for a new building to be finished in early 1980. The new building, consistent with Seestadt's planning input, would have a computer operations room in the basement equipped with liquid-cooling facilities to accommodate the larger IBM mainframes. Eastern's current building had no such facili-ties but, since the present IBM mainframes are air-cooled, this made no difference. As alternatives were generated to solve the CPU capacity problem, he knew that the air- versus liquid-cooling issue could be important. At Eastern's pre-sent location, the addition of facilities for liquid cooling would involve major construction to raise the ceiling sub-stantially.

Mr. Seestadt now had two problems that he knew interacted with one another: the short-run CPU capacity problem and a later move of all computing facilities to a new building. He could not help but wonder if any of the alternatives generated by the team working on the short-run problem might not be consistent with the longer-run situation.

ALTERNATIVE SOLUTIONS--1

On Monday, October 17, 2 days before the meeting scheduled with Mr. Seestadt to go over alternative solutions to the capacity planning problem, the team met in Mr. Gullickson's office to prepare their presentation. At that time, the team generated eight alternatives:

1. Improve applications software efficiency.
2. Rent outside computer time.
3. Split the online environment in a different manner between systems A and B.
4. Install a third 370/158.
5. Acquire an attached processor (and add-on memory) for one of the 370/158s.
6. Replace one 370/158 with an IBM 370/165 model 2.
7. Replace both 370/158s with an IBM 370/168 model 3.
8. Replace one or both 370/158s with an Amdahl 470/V6.

In discussing these alternatives, the team decided to eliminate the first as being very costly and questionable regarding its outcome. They also eliminated rearranging the applications between systems. Ms. Robinson had established that with or without Taco Bell reservations, there was no way to switch the applications around between the two systems. Thus, any alternative presented would involve some type of hardware solution.

The team members also discussed the fact that going to a non-IBM alternative, such as option 8, would be looked upon as very risky by several of the company's senior managers, especially if both 370 machines were replaced by an Amdahl machine. The team members, especially Said Motamed, felt that this alternative was, from a technical perspective, very attractive. Motamed stressed the fact that no software or file-conversion problems would be encountered with the conversion to Amdahl and that the switch could be made in a matter of days. Explaining this and selling the conversion idea to senior management, the team members knew, would be a difficult task. In the end, they decided to present this alternative at last to Mr. Seestadt.

On Wednesday of that week, Mr. Seestadt listened with interest to the team's presentation of alternatives. After hearing them, he responded with some "top of the head" reactions. In summary, they were as follows.

The 370/168-3 and the Amdahl 470/V6 options would leave Eastern with only one CPU, and he was concerned with the desirability of having no backup machine for emergencies, especially in view of the critical nature of the reservations application. He was very concerned with the Eastern reservation system—a reservations outage was much more severe from a business perspective than any other type of systems failure. Since the acquisition of the second 370/158, Eastern had the capability of switching the reservations software to system B in the event of an outage on system A. The switch took place when the outage was determined likely to exceed 4 hours. Although it had not been necessary to switch in the past 5 months, there were four such outages in 1976, averaging 9 hours each. The second CPU had eliminated 20 hours of downtime in 1976.

Coupled with the downtime problem was the fact that the 360/165 and 370/168 are liquid-cooled machines. The computer room in the new building can accommodate such facilities, but the problems associated with modifying existing space (expense plus the downtime or rental of computer time) made him reject these alternatives. Thus, Seestadt reasoned that the viable options to analyze and present to management were: (4) a third 370/158, (5) an attached processor for one of the present 370/158s, and (3) and IBM-compatible mainframe, probably an Amdahl. Mr. Seestadt scheduled a meeting with Messrs. Gullickson and Curry to discuss these three options further.

ALTERNATIVE SOLUTIONS—2

On Friday, October 28, 1977, the meeting between Seestadt, Gullickson, and Curry took place. Mr. Curry's staff had done some analysis of the technical considerations associated with each option and presented the following.

370/158-3

Eastern's operations room is quite small and currently very cramped. Along the far wall, there are six small offices for operators and programmers which would have to be torn down to make room for another CPU. It is not yet known where the displaced personnel would be relocated. A third 158 would require the acquisition of the following equipment and personnel:

1	158-3 CPU
1	1270 Memorex communications device
2-4	disk spindles
3-4	tape drives
1	card reader
4	CRTs
1	printer (possibly)
1	systems programmer
1	systems analyst
4	operators

Extra software products for the third CPU would cost an additional $2500 per month, and there would be a one-time installation expense of $50,000 (not including any computer room construction). Mr. Curry's staff pointed out that the level of complexity involved in tying together three CPUs is substantially greater than with two, but no severe problems were anticipated.

If this option is chosen, Eastern will run Eastern reservations on system A, Easy-Lodge and Taco Bell on system B, and everything else on the new machine, system C.

Attached Processor

The attached processor (AP) is a relatively new development proposed by IBM for users with problems similar to Eastern's. Customer shipments of APs for 158s began in September 1977, and there is therefore very little user experience to assist Eastern in evaluating the AP. An AP unit shares main memory with the host CPU, but has no input-output channels; all I/O is executed through the channels of the host. IBM estimates a 70-90 percent increase in throughput.

Mr. Curry's staff has identified several hardware modifications and a major software conversion that would accompany this option. The attached processor runs only with the MVS operating system, requiring Eastern to engage in a rapid conversion to MVS from its current VS1 operating system. This is estimated to be a 9 person-month project. MIS management feels that the conversion could be accomplished in 4 months, at a cost of $27,000, but only if absolutely necessary. The MVS system extension (software for the AP) leases for $1000 per month above the cost of MVS itself, which would not be significantly different from that of VS1.

An additional megabyte of memory is required for each CPU over and above the AP to accommodate the more complex MVS operating system. Furthermore, system A has somehow acquired some Control Data memory over the years, and this needs to be replaced with IBM memory prior to the AP installation. The total one-time cost for all hardware modifications is estimated to be $49,000.

The AP unit would need one-third the space required by a third 370/158. The space is not currently available. No additional personnel would be required, but the following equipment would be necessary:

1   attached processor
3   megabyte memory
1   1270 Memorex communications device
1   tape spindle
2   tape drives
3   CRTs

$3500 per month of extra software product would also be required.

If this option is implemented, system A would run Easy-Lodge and Taco Bell reservations, and system B with the AP would run Eastern reservations and everything else. Capacity is estimated to be sufficient through 1979.

Amdahl 470V/6

Although Mr. Curry's staff was still investigating the Amdahl alternative, they were able to report that the Amdahl corporation could deliver a 470V/6 by February 1978 with no difficulty. It would utilize Eastern's software, file structures, and peripheral equipment with no problems. Amdahl would support all IBM software. No additional peripherals would be needed in the short-term, although a $75,000 pulse-leveling motor generator would be required. No additional personnel would be hired. The 470/V6 would supply Eastern with a CPU capacity of roughly 30 million transactions per month.

The conversion effort would require the same space as a third 370/158, since all three machines would need to be in the operations room during conversion. Eastern could then do what it pleased with the 370/158s, but would be dependent on the one CPU in terms of reliability. The Amdahl is an air-cooled machine.

At the conclusion of the meeting, all three attendees promised to do some more thinking about the viability of the three options. It was agreed that Mr. Seestadt would be responsible for choosing an option to recommend to senior management, but that the other two would be available for support or to react to Seestadt's ideas.

INPUT FROM IBM

Mr. Seestadt had hardly returned to his office when he received a telephone call from Harold Ray, one of the IBM representatives on the Eastern account. He requested a meeting with Mr. Seestadt to discuss the Eastern computer capacity problem. The meeting was set for Wednesday, November 2, 1977.

Harold Ray and his colleague, Carol Jasperson, met with Mr. Seestadt. They had also been present during the October 10 discussion of the transactions growth forecasts. They expressed the view that since Eastern is running an IBM shop, IBM has an obligation to assist Eastern in solving their short-term capacity problem. Mr. Seestadt also knows that IBM is concerned about the possibility of an IBM-compatible machine being installed to replace the present IBM equipment.

The IBM representatives suggested that, in their opinion, an AP unit is Eastern's best alternative at this time. The AP, they claimed, would provide sufficient capacity for the next 2 years, and the conversion to the MVS operating system upgrade would only benefit Eastern in the long run. Mr. Seestadt admitted to having an interest in MVS; it would provide his systems programmers with an online interaction capability (TSO) that is not present in VS1. In fact, Eastern had already planned an MVS upgrade following the

eventual installation of updated mainframes, but Mr. Seestadt was convinced that this upgrade would also be desirable if Eastern acquired the Amdahl. At the conclusion of
the meeting, Mr. Seestadt thanked them for their concern,
and promised to let them know Eastern's decision on this
matter as soon as possible.

On Friday, November 12, 1977, Mr. Seestadt sat contem-
plating a list of general business considerations that he
felt were important when considering how to solve the short-
run capacity problem **and** the longer-run situation (especially in terms of long-term needs to support growth), including
the fact that a new building and computer room were coming.
He thought about a number of factors including:

The manner and timing of a potential reduction in IBM support
The viability of Amdahl as a long-term hardware manufacturer
in light of possible IBM marketing and engineering stra-
tegies to limit the impact of hardware-compatible vendors
The impact of recruiting and retaining systems programmers
The risks involved in being a single CPU environment if both
158s were to be released
The risk to Eastern's "image" of being a non-IBM installation

To complicate matters further, Eastern has had a long-
standing contract with IBM to provide hotel service for
IBM's traveling personnel at a slightly reduced rate. Eastern does this for other companies as well, and Mr. Seestadt
is confident that this is a good arrangement for IBM and
will, therefore, not be affected by the hardware decision
that he will recommend. He also knows that any decision to
switch to Amdahl could make him a corporate scapegoat should
IBM terminate the contract arrangement for any reason.

It is late in the evening and Robert Seestadt is chewing
on an old cigar butt while thinking about life in general and
his three hardware options in particular. His wife has gone
to bed, and the ice cubes in his drink have melted. Eastern
has 3 to 4 months to implement a decision. He must meet
with his staff early in the morning to pick a strategy to be
recommended to senior management.

ASSIGNMENT

1. What should Eastern do? Discuss the pros and cons of each alternative and justify your choice on the basis of Eastern's short-term situation as well as its long-term needs. Include both the technical and political considerations in making your recommendations.

INTRODUCTION

The computer doesn't work! Installed only 14 months ago, the computer has not given the Fosday Company the information that was promised.

The reports are late.
The information is not accurate.
The formats of the reports are not usable.
The information required from the various departments is difficult to obtain.
The data processing department is always late completing its work.

Something has to be done! The company must have the information it needs to remain competitive. As a result, the president of the company has called a meeting of the department managers to develop a plan to "salvage" the investment already made in data processing equipment and labor hours. The objective of the meeting is to develop a plan to present to the executive committee, which meets in 3 weeks. The committee has been concerned with the high expenditures in the data processing area and would like to know how a return on that investment can be realized.

The president of the Fosday Company has selected the attendees: president, vice president, treasurer–controller, assistant controller (also the data processing manager), purchasing manager, inventory control manager, and the plant manager.

Company Background

The Fosday Company is a paper product wholesaler with approximately $30 million in annual sales. This is an increase of over 20 percent a year over the past 5 years. Founded 9 years ago, the company is family–owned. Most of the employees have been with the company since the beginning. However, increased sales have required new employees to be hired within the past year. The purchasing manager is relatively new in his position and the old-time employees question his ability to handle the job.

Fosday is primarily a wholesaler, so there is a limited amount of manufacturing. The only manufacturing is to cut paper into smaller sheet sizes or to cut roll paper supplies into sheets. Other facts about the Fosday Company are:

1. Profits	4.2 percent
2. Market share	40 percent
3. Long-term debts	Substantial
4. Financial condition	Fair but much improved
5. Warehouses	Cleveland, Ohio
	Dayton, Ohio
6. Subsidiaries	Detroit, Michigan ($10 million)
	Albany, New York ($7 million)
	Seattle, Washington ($14 million)
	Dallas, Texas ($13 million)
	Columbia, Missouri ($3 million)
7. Pending acquisitions	Milwaukee, Wisconsin ($13 million)
	Portland, Oregon ($5 million)
8. Corporate objectives	Establish inventory turnover rate to 5 to 6 times a year
	Increase profit margin by maintaining price structure and reducing expenditures

Maintain customer service levels at 90 percent (to stockout conditions)
Provide flexible information systems in order to facilitate corporate expansion
Improve cash-flow position

9. Employees   50
10. Salespeople   25

Data Processing at Fosday

The computer data processing installation was proposed 2 years ago by the treasurer/controller in order to meet the needs of the rapidly expanding company.

The assistant controller was assigned responsibility (in addition to his previous responsibilities) for managing the computer data processing department. This included purchase, modification, and implementation of computer applications available from the hardware vendor. Substantial progress has been made since the computer was installed 14 months ago. The user departments do not have sufficient time to assist data processing in implementing computer processing applications, so the application systems have been purchased from the computer vendor. However, no help has been requested for installing them.

The computer data processing department has the following:

1. Computer equipment
     Minicomputer (1 Mbyte memory)
     2 disk drives (200 Mbytes of online storage)
     1 printer (300 lpm)
     2 tape drives
     5 CRT terminals
2. Employees
     1 manager (assistant controller)
     2 programmers
     2 operators
     2 data entry operators
     2 control clerks

3. Computer system installed

    <u>Order entry system</u>

    The sales orders are entered into the computer via a CRT terminal. The information is reasonably accurate, but the reports are usually received after the orders have been shipped.

    <u>Purchasing system</u>

    The purchasing system information is available to purchasing through a CRT terminal in the purchasing department. Purchasing is not sure whether the information is accurate, and the reports are not used. Most purchase orders are input to the computer under blanket purchase order numbers, and changes in these orders have not been forwarded to data processing.

    <u>Inventory control system</u>

    The inventory control system is completely inaccurate. The inventory values are wrong, and there is no indication when inventories are removed from stock to be cut. Stock values are increased by purchase orders and decreased by sales orders and adjustments.

    <u>General accounting</u>

    The computer contains all the information relative to accounts payable and accounts receivable. The information has substantial use. The information is assumed to be accurate, although no one is sure.

4. Budgets

Equipment	$ 78,600	(purchase)
Software	63,500	(purchase)
Salaries	79,200	(annual)
Supplies	36,200	(annual)
Maintenance	8,000	(annual)
Benefits	18,000	(annual)
	$283,500	

5. Data processing objectives

    Use the CRT terminals more effectively.

    Increase the computer capability by 40 percent.

    Install a material requirements planning system by year end.

    Decrease turnaround time for the computer reports.

    Hire one more programmer and one data entry operator by year end.

Profiles of Personnel to Be at the Meeting

Company president. The president has been in the paper business for over 40 years. He started the company in 1974 with only two other people (a warehouser and a salesperson). What little management experience he has was gained over the past 10 years. His business philosophy is to operate at the company's upper credit limit and to acquire complementary subsidiaries whenever possible. As a result, the company is profitable but operates from financial crisis to financial crisis.

The president has no knowledge of electronic data processing and does not want to get involved with its implementation. However, the computer salesperson has convinced him that the computer can solve many of his company problems, so he has decreed that electronic data processing will be implemented and used.

Company vice president. The president's son, the vice president was hired only recently. He has an MBA degree but virtually no experience. He is expected to be the next president. He is convinced that electronic data processing is necessary to be competitive.

The primary fault he can see in the data processing department is a lack of planning and a failure to notify top management as to how schedules are being completed. He would like to get more involved in the planning process for the data processing department but knows very little about the computer.

Treasurer (controller). The company treasurer/controller is a CPA hired 6 years ago. He is a major reason why the company has remained in business. His business knowledge is excellent and his personableness has kept many creditors from foreclosing on company debts.

Although he is not an expert in data processing, he has assumed the responsibility for the data processing department and has made all decisions regarding the data processing. This includes equipment selection (i.e., computer, CRT display devices, disks, etc.) and applications programs (i.e., accounts receivable, accounts payable, purchasing, inventory control, etc.). These decisions are based on information passed to him from the data processing manager.

He also feels electronic data processing is necessary, but he recognizes that the company has received very little tangible benefit since the equipment was purchased in 1981.

Plant manager. The plant manager has been newly appointed to this position after the previous plant manager resigned. He was one of the three founders of the company and was sales manager for the past 10 years. He believes that data processing is restricting the freedom of the sales department and would like data processing to make the order entry process more flexible. Up to this time, he has not had time to work with data processing to tell them what information is needed. Although he doesn't use the reports furnished by data processing, he feels the information is accurate. At the present time, 25 percent of the sales orders are expedited and are not entered into the computer.

Inventory control manager. The inventory control manager is in charge of the warehouse operations. This includes the receipt, storage, withdrawal, and shipment of paper materials. Most of the process is retained within his head. he sees no need for paper documents to indicate shipments or receipts other than the customer order or the purchase order. He is not forcefully against the computer as long as he doesn't have to get involved with it. His main objection is that it does not agree with what he knows is right. He has not used the reports he received from data processing for the past year, although he has not talked to anyone about correcting the reports.

Purchasing manager. The purchasing manager was originally hired as a buyer 2 years ago. However, the untimely death of the previous manager placed him in the position. The previous company he worked for had substantial electronic data processing support. He has many ideas about data processing support but has no idea as to the amount of money involved. He would like to help data processing and is extremely enthusiastic when asked. However, he is seldom asked and has too much work to actively seek participation with the development of data processing systems.

He is trying to understand all the workings of the manual purchasing system and does not know all the reports that are available to him from DP. He knows that the reports he does receive are not accurate, although he will admit that all the input data is not always sent to the data processing department.

Data processing manager (assistant controller). The data processing manager has been with the company for 8 years. He set up the original accounting procedures and then was made assistant controller when the treasurer was hired. When the computer was first proposed, he was considered a natural for the data processing position. He was sent to programming school and has since learned a great deal about electronic data processing. Since his background has been in accounting, the accounting systems have worked fairly well. However, the remainder of the systems are not accurate.

For the past 2 years he has been working 10 to 14 hours a day, for 6 days a week. He has written all the programs himself, so he feels the inaccuracy of information is because he is not receiving support from the other department employees and because they are not submitting accurate input data. He has not worked with the line managers, and he is not sure what they can do to help in developing the programs. Now, he is afraid of losing his job, so he is personally monitoring all data submitted to data processing.

ASSIGNMENT

1. Evaluate the past actions of the Fosday Company in implementing and operating a computer data processing system.
2. Outline the steps that should be taken to correct the situation and to make the computer-based information system an effective support for operations and management decision making.

August 3, 1984

Gentlemen:

Horticultural Enterprises, Inc., is considering the development of an electronic data processing system to improve the efficiency of clerical and accounting functions and to begin the development of a database to aid management in decision making. HEI has decided that, because of its organizational philosophy, an in-house data processing installation is the only type of system we should consider. Our initial plans call for installation within the next 6 months, with the first two applications, payroll and general ledger, being implemented by January 1, 1985. Two additional applications, accounts payable and invoicing and accounts receivable, are scheduled for implementation by April 1, 1985. A fifth application, inventory management, is tentatively planned for later in 1985.

We are currently in the process of system selection and are scheduling initial presentations from several vendors with offices in the local area. With this in mind, we have included a copy of a Request for Proposal. If you feel that your organization can provide the system attributes that we require, then we would welcome a 1- to 1½-hour presentation on either August 13 or 16.

Within a week or two of those initial presentations, we will have narrowed our choice down to two or three vendors who appear to have best met our requirements. At that point, we will begin a more extensive screening of the remaining vendors to determine which system best meets our needs. More extensive requirements descriptions will then be made available to the remaining vendors. HEI's personnel and consultants will provide assistance to vendors where possible, as we wish to develop a long-term relationship with a supplier for our mutual benefit.

Attached as Exhibit 1 is a brief description of our organization. Exhibit 2 is a description of the applications the organization is planning in the future. Exhibit 3 is a list of criteria upon which the vendor selection will be based. It is organized according to: hardware characteristics desired, software characteristics desired, and support desired.

Sincerely,

President
Horticultural Enterprises, Inc.

Exhibit 1 Horticultural Enterprises, Inc.: Request for proposal

---

Background of HEI

A. Description of the Organization
Horticultural Enterprises, Inc., is actually the largest of four companies which would be utilizing the EDP system. All four companies are involved in the horticultural industries. Horticultural Enterprises, Inc., sells flowers, green plants, fertilizers, pots, and other supplies to retail and wholesale florists and to growers. Thomas Manufacturing sells small greenhouses, heating and cooling systems, and other equipment used by growers. Greenflower Floral is a

company with two retail florist shops in Gresham, Oregon. Figeroa Enterprises includes Quantum Plastics, a company which manufactures plastic pots for growers, and a growing range in Portland and Gresham, Oregon. Thus, there are six operating divisions in four companies.

Horticultural Enterprises, Inc., and the other companies have been growing at about 25 percent a year for the past 10 years, and we anticipate similar growth in the near future. At present, the combined sales for all the companies is in the $3 to $6 million range. Because of volume and growth rate, we need a more sophisticated system for speed, control, and information, both for present use and future growth.

B. Present processing capabilities
Presently, we are using a Firefly FX330* to run our applications. This machine is for processing only and cannot handle machine-readable files. All six payrolls are run on the FX330. Receivables, statements and aging are run for two of the companies, and payables are run for all six divisions. The FX330 provides a limited number of totals for control and management information. The general ledger is not run on the FX330, and we have no system of inventory control.

---

*An accounting machine, not a computer.

Exhibit 2 Applications required

A. Payroll
1. The payroll presently has no unique features. The majority of the people are paid by the hour, with some people on salary. However, we are planning to pay our salespeople based on a percentage of gross margin, starting some time in the next 2 years. This requires that the payroll system can be tied in to the invoicing systems in the future.
2. The payroll is run weekly. There are six separate payrolls for the separate operating divisions, with completely separate files. The total payroll for all six divisions is approximately 200. Processing would include:

    a. Weekly input of master file changes as necessary
    b. Weekly input of regular and overtime hours
    c. Weekly edit runs as necessary until weekly run is correct
    d. Weekly payroll journal and year to date
    e. Journal totals weekly creation of entries for the general journal
    f. Quarterly 941s
    g. Year W-2s

3. Major considerations for the payroll system will be security of information and security of any form on input.

B. General ledger

1. The general ledger system has no unusual requirements. There are six general ledgers for the six operating divisions. We will also need the ability to draw up consolidated statements.

2. The general ledger will be run monthly, with about 200 accounts on file in each ledger and about 40 entries per ledger per month (about 5 accounts per ledger entry). The majority of the entries come from the accounts payable system, the invoicing and accounts receivable system, and the payroll system. Other entries will be made as needed by the office manager. Besides the monthly balance sheets and income statements, we plan to run projected and interim statements at our option.

C. Invoicing and accounts receivable

1. The invoicing and accounts receivable system will be based on entering the sales orders in batches the day following creation of orders. This open order file will be used to create an open invoice file, which will then be used for updating customer accounts, analyzing sales, updating inventory, posting to general ledger, computing commissions, and creating invoice documents and statements. We also need the capability to compute gross margins; check credit; analyze sales by salesperson, customer, and product categories; age accounts receivable; use open-item or balance-forward cash posting; and generate mailing lists from the customer file.

2. The sales orders will be entered daily. Shipping documents will be checked against sales orders daily, with appropriate orders used to create open invoices. A sales analysis will be run daily and monthly. Statements and invoices will be run monthly, with several management reports run after month-end. There are three divisions that will use order entry. The average number of orders for the three divisions combined is about 125 per day, with a peak of about 200 per day. There are an average of 1000 statements per month, with a peak of about 1300 at month-end. About 2000 to 3000 invoices, with about 5 line items each, will need to be printed for mailing to the customers. The total customer file currently is about 3500 customers.

D. Accounts payable

1. The accounts payable system will be based on entering purchase orders into an open PO file as soon as the orders are written. All other documents will be matched manually and payment approved before entry into the system for payment. The purchase orders will also provide input into the inventory management system and general ledger. Virtually all disbursements except payroll will be issued through the accounts payable system.

2. We process about 900 invoices a month for all six divisions combined. The file will consist of approximately 600 vendors with about 500 checks a month being issued. Processing will include:
   a. Daily entry of newly created purchase orders
   b. Weekly runs projecting cash needs from the open PO file and listing open POs that require follow-up
   c. Weekly check runs creating checks and transactions file for the general ledger
   d. Monthly and yearly runs of volume and gross margin by vendor by product

E. Inventory management

1. Initially, the inventory system will be for developing a history of our volumes and turnover. As a distribution organization, we have our major investment in inventory. Therefore, the historical reports must emphasize turnover, gross margins, volumes by vendors, overstocks, reorder points, and other information that will improve our utiliza-

tion of inventory dollars. In addition, information from the inventory file must be used for online input edits for pricing purposes. As the system and our confidence in it develop, we will enter orders online and depend on the system to advise us of out-of-stocks immediately. We will also need gross margins to compute salespeople's commissions and for certain management reports.

2. We have a unique problem in inventory management in our cut flower department. The price of cut flowers changes daily. Also, each day a flower sits in our cooler, the price drops. The older flowers are not necessarily sold first, so determining the price of flowers and keeping an accurate inventory presents a formidable problem. We require some sort of automatic aging of inventory, with price changes.

3. Other than cut flowers, our inventory control presents no unusual problems. We plan to include a summary of inventory sold by category (not individual item) on the daily sales report (see invoicing and accounts receivable). In addition, we will print a daily inventory exception report listing items we should buy, and weekly, monthly, and yearly stock-status report. We anticipate putting 2000 items on file initially, and adding cut flowers later. Any miscellaneous items will be entered manually by category. We will have inventory grouped into approximately 100 categories.

In addition to the initial applications, Horticultural Enterprises, Inc., is considering applications for future use. While the hardware and software probably will not be sophisticated enough to handle these applications initially, the expandability of the system at low cost to handle these applications in the future will be a consideration in the final decision. The list of applications is roughly in order of our present priorities.

F. Future applications desired
1. 15 percent increase in transaction volume per year for 5 years
2. Online order entry—requires a terminal 250' from mainframe and slow-speed print capability in addition to main printer
3. Ability to create input and receive hard-copy output at Gresham, Oregon, and Portland, Oregon

4. Timesharing capabilities for managers--inquiry and simple programming
5. Generation of dunning letters to customers--type quality, neatness, and availability of upper- and lower-case type are a consideration.

ASSIGNMENT

1. Prepare Exhibit 3. This should provide, in a form to which a vendor can react, the information each vendor should provide to HEI about the system they propose. Divide the information into four categories: hardware, software, support, and miscellaneous. Following are some examples:

Hardware: The amount of main memory proposed, the total amount of memory that can be supported by this system, the size of increments of memory that can be added, and the cost of each increment.

Software: The compilers (interpreters) available on the system, the cost of each, and the maintenance cost (if any).

Support: The training courses available, the cost and locations of each.

2. Comment on the vendor selection procedure being used by HEI. How, if at all, would you change it?

As one of its diverse activities, the Maxim Holding Company controls several large commercial cleaning plants throughout the United States. These plants are all quite large (200+ employees) and do approximately the same type of work.

Each plant has several work centers. The procedure was to move workers from work center to work center as the work load fluctuated. The workers could be classed as very low skilled, and there was heavy turnover and absenteeism. In all plants, substitute workers were often used when work load demanded additional persons. Each plant worked all three shifts, and the operations of each were controlled by a shift manager. Several foremen, each from one of the work centers, report to a shift manager.

The cleaning plants were characterized by animosity between the workers and management. Each plant was unionized, and in the past, the union and the management had had bitter fights concerning promotion of employees, salaries, and the introduction of automated equipment. In discussing what they liked about their jobs, employees most often responded with "nothing" or by mentioning the security of the job and its fringe benefits (obtained by the union through negotiation).

One aspect of the job was a system of measuring work-center productivity. The nature and number of items passing through each work center were recorded by the workers. Also, each worker punched in and out of each work center, which allowed calculation of total work-center labor time on each shift. Combination of these two figures resulted in a measure of worker productivity in a work center. This data was used by management to evaluate foremen and to estimate future requirements.

At the headquarters of the Maxim Company, the technical staff of the information systems department convinced top management that an automated information system could be developed to replace the manual productivity measurement system. It was decided that because of superior employees (in education and training), the Seattle plant would be the prototype for such a system.

The information systems staff at headquarters designed the system, programmed it, and set up classes for instructing the Settle personnel in its use. Union officials had been assured that no jobs would be lost because of the new system. The only major job change was the elimination of the timekeeper position. Under the old manual system, timekeepers passed through the work centers picking up time and volume data from cards kept by the workers and foremen. The senior employees who held this job were to be reassigned to correcting errors that might be present when the automated system was running.

Soon, badge-reading source recorders used to input employee data and electronic scales used to input the work volume data were installed in the Seattle plant slightly in advance of the instruction classes for employees. At the classes, employees were shown how to punch in using a badge card in a source recorder. Each time they changed work station, they had to punch out on one recorder and in on another in the station into which they moved. Also, as cleaned items passed through a work center, they were grouped and weighted by the employees. The employee and volume data were recorded online on the plant's computer and daily productivity reports were provided to foremen, the shift managers, and the plant managers. The total plant payroll function was also performed by the prototype system.

One week after the employee classes on how to use the equipment, the new system was put into use. During the shake down of the new system, the old procedure was also used in parallel.

ASSIGNMENT

1. Discuss the following:
(a) How workers and managers reacted to the new system in terms of attitudes, actions, and behavior.
(b) Why these reactions occurred.
2. How, if you had been a consultant to the Maxim Holding Company, would you have done things differently regarding the system and its installation?

Mead-Bond Engineering is an engineering construction firm specializing in large commercial buildings. They have an international reputation for designing modernistic office buildings which provide distinctive corporate headquarters.

The emergence of information systems at Mead-Bond Engineering was similar to that of most organizations. Mead-Bond initially put up its major accounting applications followed with personnel systems. Then it implemented a variety of mainstream applications, including inventory management and contracts, and eventually moved into engineering graphics. Information systems have historically been a centralized function at Mead-Bond Engineering with most processing done on a large-scale IBM computer system. In the mid-1970s, minicomputers began to emerge within the engineering groups of Mead-Bond Engineering. Since these computers were used primarily for specialized engineering applications, they created very little concern for information systems management, and were for the most part ignored by top management. In the early 1980s, the advent of the personal computer resulted in a proliferation of personal computers in all functional areas of the organization.

Information systems management became concerned about the widespread purchasing of personal computers and, in some respects, viewed them as a threat to the centralized information systems function. In an attempt to address the situation, information systems management approached the information systems steering committee and suggested that all purchases of either minicomputers or personal computers be approved by the information systems function. This seemed reasonable to the steering committee, and the policy was implemented.

However, it quickly became clear that such authority was of little value. Whenever end-users wanted to buy a particular device, if they could not get it approved by information systems, they resorted to political tactics and could argue that information systems really shouldn't be deciding whether an end-user could make a $3000 or $4000 purchase. If that tactic didn't work, end-users would simply go underground and make their purchases discretely enough that they would go undetected by information systems. As a result, the proliferation of end-user computing continued at a prolific rate.

The managers at Mead-Bond, including the information systems managers, were busy enough with other issues to not be too concerned with the proliferation of computers throughout the organization. By the mid-1980s there was one computer for every 2½ employees at Mead-Bond Construction. Then the problems began.

A financial analyst, using a financial modeling language, made a recommendation on a building procurement decision. The analyst was reasonably experienced at using the language; however, in this case he made a slight error in the way he constructed some computations. The result was that the analysis indicated a much more favorable financial profile for the purchase than was actually true. As a result, the company lost $250,000 a year for 3 years until it could see the property. Needless to say, management was very upset and some anticomputer sentiment emerged.

Several end-users had bought a variety of personal computers to support such things as office automation, financial modeling, and engineering analysis. After using these computers for several months, they began to realize that they would need to connect to the central computer to get access to much of the data they needed to support their decision making. However, when they attempted to connect to the computer, they found that their hardware and software were incompatible with the processing environment used by information systems. The only way they could achieve interface was to replace the equipment they had purchased with new equipment at considerable financial expense. This upset a lot of budgets and a lot of managers.

The information systems department began to work on establishing a telecommunications network to support a variety of terminals and personal computing devices for direct access to corporate data. They went through a financial forecast to determine how much it would cost to upgrade to the new processing environment. The original estimates indicated that the total upgrade, including a mainframe upgrade, would run approximately $4 million. Management approved the upgrade and implementation began. However, as they began final plans for implementation, users began to "come out of the woodwork" raising concerns about how the PCs and terminals they had been using for the past several years would interface to the new processing environment. For the most part, information systems had been unaware of many of the users' devices and their access to the central computer and had made no provisions for a migration strategy to ensure that they would be compatible. The diverse variety of user interfaces would require the purchase of additional communications software and hardware. The additional total expenditure was a half a million dollars.

The accumulative effect of these three incidents resulted in top management becoming very upset with the information systems department and questioning them as to how they had let this fiasco happen.

Mr. Al Napier, vice president of information systems, responded in a memo to Mr. Richard Scammel, executive vice president and chairman of the steering committee, and explained that information systems didn't "just" let this happen. He resurrected the memos and statements from several years earlier, which indicated that no end-user was to purchase equipment without clearing it with information systems. Mr. Napier explained that this policy had never been adhered to, that end-users overrode information systems' authority, or simply took their purchases underground and did whatever they pleased, and that now this violation of the policy was catching up with the organization.

This response was not satisfactory to either Mr. Scammel or any members of the steering committee. They rather angrily responded, saying "Don't use old memos to cover up your lack of leadership. We look to you for providing leadership in information systems, and this problem has been going on for some time now. The only constructive thing that information systems has done is sit on a 5-year-old policy that obviously was not satisfactory to take care of the issue."

Mr. Napier and his staff got very upset by the position of top management and felt they had been unfairly treated. In discussing the situation with their information systems colleagues in other organizations, they found that similar problems had emerged, but not nearly as serious as the one Mr. Napier was facing.

Mr. Napier realizes that management is going to need a scapegoat for this problem and that information systems managers are very good scapegoats. Arguing is not going to do much good.

The next week, Mr. Napier receives a memo from Mr. Scammel, directing him to come up with an action plan to correct the end-user computer dilemma. Specifically, he is instructed to resolve the problem of incompatible equipment and the quality problems with end-user software such as was experienced with the financial model used in the procurement decision. Further, Mr. Napier is told to have the action plan documented and available for the steering committee within a week.

ASSIGNMENT

1. Develop an action plan that includes policies and courses of action to resolve the problem that developed at Mead-Bond Engineering.
2. In hindsight, what positive initiatives could Mr. Napier and the information systems staff have taken to have avoided the unpleasant situation that developed?

National Retailing, Inc., is one of the nation's largest retail organizations. The corporation has divisions in markets such as department stores, low-margin stores, jewelry stores, book stores, and clothing stores.

Many corporate functions within each division are performed centrally from the company's headquarters in St. Louis. The retail buying function is one of those centralized functions.

A RETAIL BUYING SYSTEM EVOLVES

In late March 1979, personnel from the corporate data processing staff were requested to meet with the corporate director of marketing research and the divisional merchandising manager of the department store division. The subject was a decision support system to be used by the central buying staff to assist in their annual planning. An initial meeting was held with the director of data processing and the manager of systems design. Two other meetings followed in which the marketing managers met with a systems project leader and an analyst.

At the first meeting, the two marketing managers pointed out that other departments in the company were successful users of DP and that since DP charges were allocated to the marketing function, they thought it would be a good idea to use some of the services for which they were paying. The director of market research had recently returned from a meeting in which decision support systems (DSS) had been discussed. He suggested that a DSS might be very useful in lessening the awful burden on buyers during the semiannual planning process.

Following the initial meeting, the systems project leader and the analyst had several other meetings with buyers to determine how buyers planned and what formal reports were used in the planning process. It was decided that a proto-type DSS would be built and tested on the company's small timesharing system and, when it was satisfactory, moved to the main computer and made available to all buyers.

Historical data were gathered from three departments, and a model was built by the analyst and then tested by one buyer from each department. Those buyers used a teletype terminal at their desks in an interactive planning mode. The tests with the buyers were conducted late in 1979. The system went through several modifications based upon buyer suggestions and was judged ready to be implemented on a full-scale basis in early 1980.

THE PLANNING SYSTEM

It is far beyond the scope of this short case to describe in detail the DSS that ultimately evolved. Still, the reader should have some appreciation of what is done by the system. National's department store division uses a top-down fore-casting approach, in which the forecast of sales in dollars for each department for the coming season is set by top management in consultation with divisional merchandise managers and buyers. The dollar estimate is called the "management plan" for the season's sales for the buyer's department. There are two 6-month planning seasons—spring and fall. The sales planning task is to divide the manage-ment plan for a season among: (1) each of the six department stores; (2) each of seven or eight classes of goods carried in each department; and (3) each of the 6 months of the season. A National department store buyer is responsible for sales, gross margin, and net profit for one or more departments in all six stores.

The buyer plans, orders, and controls all merchandise inventories. In the process, the buyers develop and execute a complete marketing and promotional plan for the departments for which they are responsible. A typical National buyer must develop separate sales dollar estimates for six stores, about eight classes, and 6-month periods broken down to each of 26 weeks. Thus, a total of 6 x 8 x 26 = 1248 estimates are required. A computer program breaks the months into weeks based upon historical patterns so that only 288 estimates are actually made by the buyers. These detailed sales estimates are the basis of weekly and monthly status reports that are given to buyers that compare actual sales with planned sales.

The onerous nature of the planning task becomes apparent when it is recognized that the sum of all the 288 variables must equal the management plan. The buyer uses historical information on sales in previous seasons, modified by judgment on future conditions, to make the sales estimate for each variable. If a buyer develops a series of estimates that sum to the management plan and then wants to change the value of any variable, problems occur. The one change triggers a series of other changes that are required to keep the sum of all variables equal to the management plan. The net effect was that, prior to the DSS, a buyer who was pressed for time tended to settle for the quickest series of estimates that would balance the plan with the management plan.

The DSS that was developed had, as one objective, the purpose of relieving the buyer from the computation associated with planning so that more time could be spent on planning itself. In the interviewing process, the systems analyst discovered that a great deal of flexibility was required of the DSS to incorporate individual differences in planning procedures used by various buyers. As a result, several estimating options were made available. Included were:

Sales will be distributed next year in the same percentages as in similar periods last year.

Each store's estimates may be put in individually.

Some stores may be entered individually and others in accordance with last year's pattern.

In addition, many options were made available to buyers for past sales data upon which to estimate. To add a touch of humor to the planning process, the systems analyst set the interactive program up as a conversation with "Herman." The following is an example of how Herman calls a buyer's attention to some present store estimates.

WHAT IS THE MANAGEMENT PLAN FOR THIS DEPARTMENT FOR THE NEXT SEASON? PLEASE PUT IN THE DOLLAR SALES IN THOUSANDS OF DOLLARS AND THEN PRESS CR.

HERMAN CALLS YOUR ATTENTION AT THE SUMMARY GIVEN BELOW.

NOTE THAT THE SALES FIGURES ARE IN THOUSANDS OF DOLLARS

A. LAST SEASON'S TOTAL SALES = 919.6
B. MANAGEMENT PLAN = 100.0
C. ADDITIONAL SALES TO ACHIEVE MANAGEMENT PLAN = 88.4
D. PERCENTAGE CHANGE OVER THE LAST SEASON'S SALES = 8.74

TABLE 1 SALES FIGURES FOR EACH OF THE STORES FOR THE NEXT SEASON ASSUMING UNIFORM GROWTH IN SALES FIGURES OF THE STORES EQUAL TO THAT SHOWN IN (D) ABOVE.

	LAST SEASON	NEXT SEASON	DIFF	PERCENT CHANGE
STORE A	371.8	404.3	32.5	8.74
STORE B	103.7	112.8	9.1	8.74
STORE C	191.4	208.1	16.7	8.74
STORE D	89.6	97.4	7.8	8.74
STORE E	87.5	95.2	7.7	8.74
STORE F	75.6	82.2	6.6	8.74
COMB	919.6	1000.0	80.4	8.74

Once store estimates were felt to be as desired, a buyer could move on to divide each store's sales into classes. This procedure would also be computer-aided.

REACTIONS AND RESULTS

After exhaustive tests by the three buyers, the system was deemed ready for conversion to the company's central computer system and made available to all 50 buyers. Final comments by the three test buyers to the systems analyst indicated that:

The DSS relieved them of routine arithmetic calculations, thereby giving them more time.

They understood what the computer was doing when they left some estimates out of their plans, so that the computer could pro-rate the balance of uncommitted dollars.

In general, they felt they understood the system and could control it; there was no evidence of oversophistication. They were delighted.

At this time, it was discovered that the central computer (which used VM/CMS) had very limited timesharing capacity left. Thus, DP made a decision to implement the full system in a batch mode. A programmer was assigned to convert the timesharing version to a batch mode written in PL/1. The divisional merchandising manager wrote the following memo to his vice president:

> You may be interested to know that we have taken the computer-assisted planning system and experimented with it in several of our departments. We are committed to using a batch system rather than a timesharing terminal. The results of our experiment have led us to widening the experiment for our fall 1981 sales plans. The batch system is a very simple one and requires the buyer to put computer input information on a form provided by our planning department. I am sure that we will continue to expand the usage of this concept.

In the summer of 1983, a university professor who knew that National had implemented a DSS, decided to check out the results. He discovered that the merchandising manager involved had since left the company to become an executive with a competitor that was also located in St. Louis.

The professor could find no evidence of the DSS at National. It was as though the planning model had never existed. The buyers were all planning manually as before.

He even had difficulty finding out exactly when the model's use had faded or if the batch version of the model had ever been made available to the buyers.

When contacted, the former merchandising manager said, "I think that the model was implemented in batch with some superficial changes added, but I really can't remember." At present, additional information is being sought about the model's demise, but knowledgeable sources are difficult to locate.

ASSIGNMENT

1. What in your opinion caused this DSS effort to fail?
2. Detail specifically changes you would make in the systems design and development procedure that would have enhanced the system's chances of being used by all the buyers.

INTRODUCTION

In the spring of 1982, Mr. Roger Kramm of Perigee Industries set out to acquire a consultant to assist his organization in developing a 5-year data processing plan. Mr. Kramm had served with Perigee for 18 months in the capacity of a systems analyst attached to the corporate staff. It was his opinion that since the company had grown dramatically during the past few years by way of acquisition and planned substantial future growth, a comprehensive data processing plan ought to be developed which would result in a system tailored to the organization's future needs.

BACKGROUND

Perigee Industries is a holding company headquartered in modern office facilities in Richardson, Texas (a suburb of Dallas). Actually, the corporate office staff is small, about 11 persons including Mr. Kramm and the clerical staff. Others located at the corporate office include:

John Turcotte, President, Perigee Industries
Jeff Farr, Senior VP, Branch Operations Division

Kevin Anderson, VP, Plastics Manufacturing Division
Tim Kohler, VP and Controller, Branch Operations Division
Michael Hassel, VP and Treasurer, Perigee Industries
Thomas Klein, VP and Controller, Perigee Industries
Alan Hunter, Staff Accounting Analyst, Perigee Industries

An organization chart of Perigee Industries is given in Figure 1.

At the end of their fiscal year ending February 1982, Perigee Industries had sales of approximately $35 million. The company had grown to this size in just a few years time because of the entrepreneurial activity of its top management. The growth had occurred primarily through acquisition, but some of the units had grown internally as well. Basically, the growth strategy of Mr. Turcotte and his team has been to acquire small businesses in the industries covered by Perigee. The holding company's current configuration reflects the strategy.

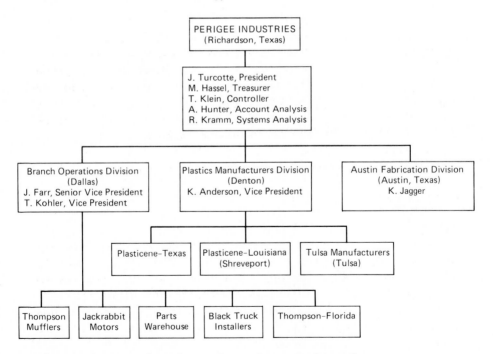

Figure 1 Organization of Perigee Industries.

BRANCH OPERATIONS DIVISION

This division consists of five free-standing businesses, each headed by a branch manager. Thompson Mufflers, the largest branch, consists of an amalgam of about 35 muffler- and car-repair shops located in Texas, Arizona, New Mexico, and Oklahoma. Jackrabbit Motors is very similar except that this firm has only seven shops, all in the metropolitan Dallas area. These two companies are separated for two reasons: customer identification and loyalty plus concerns in the antitrust area. Black Truck Istallers deals with commercial customers, primarily trucking concerns. All three of these organizations are serviced by the Parts Warehouse, which deals with other competitors as well. Finally, Thompson-Florida is a group of 10 muffler shops servicing the Miami area.

PLASTICS MANUFACTURING DIVISION

The Plastics Manufacturing Division has its headquarters in a 75,000-square-foot plant in Denton, Texas. This firm manufactures decorative plastic panels used by the building trades for office buildings and shopping centers. Another smaller facility producing similar products is in a 40,000-square-foot plant in Shreveport, Louisiana. Tulsa Manufacturing is a company acquired by Perigee Industries which makes plastic shelving for retail stores.

AUSTIN FABRICATION DIVISION

The Austin Fabrication Division consists of only one organization, Austin Fabrication. The product produced by this firm is custom interior partitions used by businesses to separate open floor space into offices. A new trend is to have open space in office buildings partitioned off to make individual or group working areas. Austin Fabrication has capitalized on this trend by producing high-quality units to order from customers all over the country.

COMPUTER FACILITIES AND PERSONNEL

Four subunits of Perigee Industries have computer processing. The major facilities are at Thompson Mufflers and Plastacene-Texas. Specifically, these units have:

Thompson Mufflers	Plastacene-Texas
XYZ 61/58	XYZ 61/58
512 Kbyte memory	64 Kbyte memory
100 Mbyte disk storage	50 Mbyte disk storage
300 lpm line printer	100 lpm line printer
200 cpm card reader	100 cpm card reader
Communications controller	

The XYZ 61/58 machines are small business computers which first appeared on the market in the mid-1970s and were acquired by the Perigee units in the 1978-79 period.

In addition, Austin Fabrication has a ZOT 11/10 with 16 k (words) of memory, 50 Mbytes of disk storage, and a 60 cps printer. An IBM PC/XT is used by Tulsa Manufacturing strictly for job estimation. Likewise, the Austin Fabrication computer is used principally for engineering applications and for estimating job costs. The Tulsa Manufacturing PC/XT is programmed by that firm's general manager and by its controller. At Austin Fabrication, a former engineer has been trained as a programmer, and this person does most of the programming. A part-time employee (a college student working summers) also assists with some programming. Both these computers are programmed in the BASIC language.

The major processing centers (Thompson Mufflers and Plastacene-Texas) each have a computer programmer. Thompson Mufflers has one keypuncher and one full-time operator. Plastacene-Texas has a single keypuncher/operator. All programming on these systems is in a subset of COBOL called Mini-COBOL.

APPLICATIONS

Thompson Mufflers had the most advanced set of applications of the two processing centers. The systems consist of general accounting, which includes general ledger, accounts payable, and accounts receivable; order entry; and sales reporting.

In addition, an online system was under development to provide perpetual inventory for the warehouse. Two CRT terminals would be used for input of inventory transactions, and a printer terminal was to be used for output at the warehouse. This system was to be implemented in June 1983.

The system at Plastacene-Texas included order entry, general accounting, and some production reporting. As with Thompson Mufflers, the accounting functions included general ledger, accounts receivable, and accounts payable.

INFORMATION SYSTEMS PLAN

Seeing that the size of Perigee Industries was growing in both number of units and sales by each unit, Roger Kramm suggested to top management that a consultant be engaged to assist in the development of a 5-year data processing plan. Mr. Kramm was troubled by the fact that the Thompson XYZ 61/58 was becoming overloaded by existing transaction volume. He knew some equipment changes would have to be forthcoming; he also knew that the equipment was obsolete technologically and should probably be replaced. He wanted to change according to a plan, however, rather than upgrading randomly. He felt that, even with the online system coming up, the system at Thompson could handle the volume through the next summer, but a change would be required before the summer of 1983.

Top management agreed, so Mr. Kramm contacted several consulting sources. To assist each potential consultant, a 2-hour discussion was held with each applicant, presenting material descriptive of Perigee Industries (similar to that given above). In addition, he provided each with the following outline.

FIVE-YEAR DATA PROCESSING MASTER PLAN

PERIGEE INDUSTRIES

What follows is a brief outline of the outputs I would expect from any consulting engagement.

1. Suggested growth pattern for systems by priority of systems. If there are alternatives, please list the strong points and weak points of each.
2. Indication of where the data processing function must be upgraded in 2 years to meet the needs of management as proposed in the 5-year projections for Perigee Industries.
3. Optimum hardware placement, first based on cost only, then my cost based on management's desires.
4. Personnel, placement, level of expertise, and any training necessary.
5. A fairly comprehensive matrix and/or chart relating the following:
   a. Process to organization
   b. Processes to application systems
   c. Application systems of data classes
   d. Data classes to organization

Again this is my plan, to be developed with the assistance of a consultant.

Kramm received proposals from several sources and, in consultation with management, selected one which follows from a well-known (but somewhat iconoclastic) management consultant. The price was somewhat lower than that bid by other consulting firms, since the lone consultant apparently had low overhead and proposed to work on the project on a part-time basis. Stretching the length of the planning study suited Perigee management since it realized that other work had to continue while the plan was being developed.

A Proposal to
PERIGEE INDUSTRIES, INC.
for the Development of
A FIVE-YEAR DATA PROCESSING MASTER PLAN
by
Management Consultant

MANAGERIAL SUMMARY

This consultant proposes to assist the personnel of Perigee Industries, Inc., in the development of a 5-year data processing master plan. The project outputs are to be a time-phased specification of computer hardware and personnel resources plus a determination of the organization's mix of computer applications. In addition, a pro-forma budget will be developed for the planned system. The project is proposed in three phases: (1) determination of the business environment and description of the current position of the organization; (2) development of the application plan; and (3) specification of the computer hardware and personnel system. A time schedule for the three phases is given, with completion forecast on August 31, 1982. A bid of $12,000 is made and broken into subsets by phase. Two intermediate management presentations are proposed. At the end of any phase, the client can decide to cancel the incompleted phases. In addition, no billings will be made to the client at the end of a phase if the consultant's work on that phase is unsatisfactory to the client.

The basis for this proposal to Perigee Industries, Inc., is two discussions with Mr. Roger Kramm. The first was a rather lengthy discussion of Perigee Industries, Inc. Concentration was upon the nature of the organization, its structure, and its use of data processing. The meeting concluded with consideration of developing a plan for the evolution of the organization's data processing and information systems. The second meeting was devoted to a discussion of how the planning project ought to be approached and what the project's outputs should be. The meeting was based upon two short, written documents directed at a preliminary description of the project. One was prepared by Mr. Kramm and one by this consultant. The proposal which follows is a synthesis of these two documents.

In order to make the proposal as clear and as specific as possible without adding unnecessary length, the following organization will be used. First, an overview statement of philosophy will discuss how the project ought to be conducted, i.e., the role of the consultant vis-a-vis Perigee Industries personnel. Next, the specific outputs of the project will be presented. The following section will discuss the procedure proposed to yield the outputs, and the proposal will conclude with the normal time and cost estimates. An appendix gives a functional flow of the project.

CONSULTING PHILOSOPHY AND APPROACH TO BE TAKEN

This consultant believes that it is the user of consulting services who is primarily responsible for a project's success. Thus, it is the user's project, not the consultant's. The role of the consultant in projects such as the one being considered here is that of advisor/doer and facilitator. The consultant does not propose to simply talk to a few people and go away to return in several months with a finished product. Rather, the project should be viewed as a joint venture between Perigee Industries, personnel and the consultant. When reading the following proposal, please note that Mr. Kramm and other personnel from Perigee Industries will be involved on a time overlap of at least 80 percent. That is, for 80 percent of the time duration of the project, we will be physically working together.

A final caveat to this consultant's philosophy concerns satisfied clients. Note that the project cost is fixed price, but it is segmented into three stages.

Client approval is required at the completion of each stage before the next stage is undertaken or the completed stage is billed. The latter practice is adopted from a colleague from the Colorado School of Mines who is a very well-known consultant, Gene Woolsey. His consulting firm is "The Rocky Mountain Fire Brigade," and its operating rule is--"If we don't put out your fire, you turn off our water." With a similar guideline, if Perigee Industries is not satisfied with the quality of work performed, no charge will be made.

PROJECT OUTPUTS

The product of this project will be a 5-year data processing and information systems plan for Perigee Industries. The plan will be composed of two interacting parts: (1) a specification of what the physical components of the system ought to be and where they should be located, and (2) a description of what applications mix ought to exist. Naturally, these will be presented in a time-phased pattern and translated into budget terms. We must provide details on:

1. A data processing/information systems plan
2. Computer hardware and software (programming languages, applications packages)
3. Personnel
4. Applications mix
5. Budget (pro forma) by year

   Characteristics of the project outputs are:

1. We must establish priorities and growth patterns.
2. We must consider various alternatives.
3. We must project that a system can
   a. Be effective in processing transactions to support business activity
   b. Provide the desired level of support for management decision making
   c. Be cost effective
   d. Be flexible and evolvable into the future (beyond 5 years)

Note that an interaction exists between the physical system components (computer hardware and personnel) and the applications mix. That is, the kind of equipment and people needed depends on what you're going to do (applications mix), but the opposite is also true. What you can do depends upon what resources you have available (equipment and personnel). For this project, we consider determination of the applications mix to be the dominant factor. Thus, a major activity of the project will be specification of the time-phased mix of applications (operational and under development) for Perigee Industries. By a time-phased applications mix, we mean that we must determine (by time period) what computer applications will be made, where, and with what interconnections. As an example, a short list of the types of systems included are:

1. Clerical systems
   Financial (e.g., payrolls, accounts receivable, accounts payable, etc.)
   Logistical (e.g., inventory, order entry, production scheduling)
2. Management control systems
   For example: cost systems, performance measuring systems, profit center measures
3. Strategic management systems
   For example: financial planning systems, merger/acquisition analysis

We must determine what types of these systems will exist within Perigee Industries over the 5-year planning horizon, and beyond. Further, we must project where these systems will be in place, when, and how they may be connected (integrated). This information plus the level of business activity (transaction volume) will allow a determination of what the hardware/software/personnel system must be in order to support the applications.

In describing the applications mix, an attempt will be made to develop a chart for Perigee Industries which relates:

1. Processes to the organization structure
2. Processes to actual applications systems
3. Application systems to data classes
4. Data classes to the organization structure

In order to project the required applications mix, we must understand Perigee Industries in terms of its current and future business environment. Thus, we must forecast or determine:

1. Growth
   Amount
   Type
2. Management style/objectives/philosophies
3. Current status
   Computer applications
   Resources (computer, personnel)
4. Business climate

In summary, the project of developing a data processing/informations systems plan will consist of the following phases and outputs:

Activity	Output
I. Assessment of organization and business environment	Description
II. Determination of applications mix	DP/IS plan
III. Hardware/software/personnel specification	Resource plan budget

See Appendix I to this proposal for a graphic description of this functional flow.

Note that the outputs of Phases II and III will be time-phased, with costs and acquisition requirements (e.g., training) specified. As the project evolves, it is possible that Phase III outputs may contain several alternatives so that Perigee management can assess cost versus managerial tradeoffs.

TIME SCHEDULE

The following time schedule shows the proposed project duration by phase. The elapsed time of each phase is projected, the real time period during which the phase is expected to occur is given, personnel involved listed, and milestones established. Also, the amount of support by the principal consultant is shown.

Phase	Activity	Project Resources	Time Period	Milestone
I (1.5 months)	Describe business environment	Consultant (8 days) Kramm Perigee management	Spring 1982	Presentation to management--buy off
II (1.5 months)	Develop applications mix	Consultant (20 days) Kramm Perigee personnel	Summer 1982	Presentation to management--buy off
III (1.5 months)	Hardware/ software/ personnel specification	Consultant (20 days) Kramm	Summer 1982	Presentation to management

The final management presentation is targeted for August 31, 1982.

It is estimated that the principal investigator will be available approximately 1 day per week through May and then 3 days per week during the summer.

COST SCHEDULE

The cost bid for the project is $12,000, composed of three phases. If the client is pleased with Phase I, a bill for $3500 will be submitted. If the client elects to continue through Phase II and is satisfied with the work, an additional $4000 will be billed. If Phase III is conducted and satisfactorily completed, a final bill for $4500 will be submitted.

All costs (report preparation, supplies, local travel, etc.) are covered within the above bid. Any travel outside of Texas or overnight lodging will be billed back to the client on a simple cost reimbursement basis. In incurring these costs, the consultant will adhere to all procedures applying to personnel of Perigee Industries.

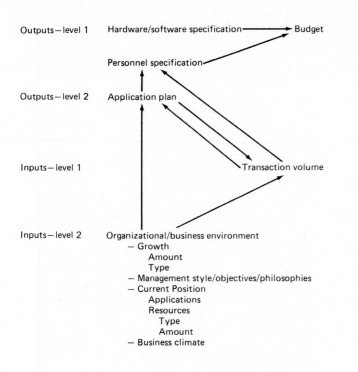

Requirements

1. Effective in processing transactions to support business activity
2. Provide desired level of support for management decision making
3. Cost effective
4. Flexible/evolvable

APPENDIX I
Perigee Industries 5-year data processing information system plan.

ASSIGNMENT

1. Discuss the wisdom of selecting a well-regarded, but somewhat different consultant. Consider that a well-known but rather expensive "Big Eight" consulting firm could have been chosen (at 5 times the cost).

2. Evaluate, in detail, the adequacy of the plan. Be specific and detail what you agree with, what you would change, and how you would make changes.

3. Evaluate the form of the consultant's proposal. Again, be specific regarding its strengths and weaknesses.

The consultant began to work with Roger Kramm in late April 1982 to conduct the first phase of the 5-year DP planning project. They began by spending a good deal of time preparing an interview schedule to be used to interview managers throughout Perigee Industries. Some time was lost from the project, however, when Roger Kramm was informed that the programmer working for Plastacene-Texas had given notice. Kramm was asked by Kevin Anderson to assist in locating a replacement. Kramm's time was also consumed by working with the programmer at Thompson Mufflers to develop the warehouse online system.

Working the scheduled 1 day per week up to mid-May, the interview schedule was completed and some interviews were done. During June, the interviews were completed, requiring some trips out of the Dallas area to several locations.

The interviewing in June went slowly for two reasons. First, Kramm was very busy working on the online system, which was scheduled to be brought up in late June. Second, the busy summer season had increased the level of the transaction volume at Thompson Mufflers to the point where a two-shift operation in the computer center was required. The consultant worked with Kramm to discuss the problem with his personnel. Consideration was given to going from the XYZ 61/58 at Thompson to a 61/60 (a 61/58 with a "front-end" communications processor) to help minimize the impact on computer processing of bringing the warehouse online (the 61/58 machine was not designed with communication in mind and therefore processed very slowly when communications were involved). The $130 a month price was attractive for an upgraded machine (the 61/60 would handle communications better), but delivery was not feasible in the required time frame. A decision was made to employ a part-time operator so Thompson could extend its data processing day.

In addition, as talks were conducted with Thompson personnel, it became apparent that the overall design of its data processing applications was awkward. A great deal of computer time was lost, for example, in correcting input errors discovered in editing. Further, it became obvious that the system would not work if the clerical personnel were not physically close to the computer. The following story illustrates the problem.

A new operator, after working a few weeks, noticed that the price being input to the computer in regard to a particular muffler seemed vastly out of line. The operator went out to a clerk to ask about the discrepancy. The clerk suggested that the price was probably for a special model, whereas the model number was likely for the standard model. When asked by the operator how to find out what was correct (the model actually installed), the response was: "Well, we could call up the customer and ask if he would crawl under his car and take a look."

The consultant took a vacation in late June while Kramm worked to bring up the warehouse system. Even upon the return of the consultant in July, nothing was done on the planning project because of difficulties that had occurred during his absence.

The online system was still not working properly. Kramm had to go to the warehouse each night to enter transactions to keep up. Furthermore, while the online system was up on the first shift, the normal batch processing of the 61/58 was degraded 120 percent. (A batch job previously taking 13 minutes to run took 28 minutes to run with the online system up.) The degradation further compounded the problems of handling the load of Thompson transactions.

The full-time operator gave notice, and took her 2-week notice as vacation time. The part-time operator went on full time.

The Thompson keypunch operator was fired (she knew the complex jobs and was very accurate) and was replaced by a temporary person.

Kramm and the Thompson Mufflers office manager were forced to work most nights and weekends to keep the system working. Because of Kramm's unavailability, the writing of the Phase I report was delayed until July 26, 1982.

By then, Plastacene-Texas had hired a new programmer/ analyst and a new full-time operator. Also somewhat helping the Thompson problem with transaction volume was the fact that the company's installers went on strike in July, thus reducing the level of business activity. The Phase I report, which was delivered to management the first week in August, summarized the results of interviews aimed at discovering the environment for which the 5-year data processing plan would be designed.

REPORT TO PERIGEE INDUSTRIES
by
Systems Counsel
Phase I Report
(1 of 3)
July 26, 1982

MANAGEMENT SUMMARY

This report covers the first phase of a three-phase consulting project for Perigee Industries. The goal of the entire project is to develop a 5-year data processing plan that will project applications, hardware and software requirements, and a time-phased budget. The project phase covered in this report is an assessment of the corporate and managerial climate in which the data processing system is to operate.

The procedure used was to conduct structured interviews with Perigee managers, to survey those persons by written questionnaire regarding their level of information satisfaction, and to hold discussions with data

processing personnel. Three general areas were inves-
tigated: (1) corporate growth, (2) data processing
resources and capability, and (3) the managerial climate.

The results of the study indicate that by the end of
the period, Perigee Industries will be about twice its
present size in terms of revenues and personnel. Furthermore, at least one new branch will be added. Data
processing transactions are forecast to exceed this
growth rate and be much more than double the present
level by the end of the period. The present two business data processing systems cannot handle the present
level of transactions adequately, let alone projected
growth. Limited personnel is a major shortcoming, with
the lack of system analysis skills being of particular
concern. Managers are generally satisfied with the
data processing system as it now exists, but all feel
that there is room for evolutionary expansion.

To summarize: Thompson Mufflers would like to run
more efficiently; Plastacene-Texas would like to undertake a major program to develop new applications; Tulsa
Manufacturing and Austin Fabrication would like to
begin business data processing applications, particularly in the inventory/production areas.

The major implications of the results for the data
processing plan are:

Thompson Mufflers will need a major system upgrade in
   the near future (1 year).
Plastacene-Texas should be enhanced in the intermediate
   time frame (1-3 years).
The plan must provide for protection against the short-
   age of data processing personnel.
High-priority new applications should be in the produc-
   tion/inventory areas.
There is a need for more managerial training in the
   data processing/interactive systems area.
There is no need for systems to be linked together.
Top management must determine authority relationships
   in regard to key data processing decisions.
By 1988, Perigee Industries will probably be spending
$500,000-$750,000 on data processing (compared with the
   present $250,000).

Problem Statement

The project proposed by this consultant and accepted by Perigee Industries is to assist in the development of a 5-year data processing master plan. The project consists of three phases: (1) determination of the business environment and a description of the current position of the organization; (2) development of the application plan; and (3) specification of computer hardware and personnel, plus a pro-forma budget. This report covers the results of phase 1 of the entire project, the "environmental assessment."

Before one can develop a data processing plan in terms of applications, equipment, and personnel, it is necessary to know the environment in which the data processing system will exist. Important questions must be answered, such as:

Where is the company going, and how fast will it grow?
What are its current data processing strengths and
    weaknesses?
How will the organization be managed, and how will the
    computer fit into the projected management style?
Does the company have the management system necessary
    to support the data processing system?
How well satisfied are the present users of the data
    processing system with its capabilities, and how
    should it evolve?

Procedure

To answer these and a variety of other questions, Roger Kramm and I conducted structured interviews with most Perigee managers and a number of personnel in subordinate positions. Figure 1 indicates the number of people interviewed at various levels of the Perigee Corporation.

Figure 1 Interview coverage

Perigee Level	1
Branch Operations Division	4
Plastic Manufacturers Division	9
Austin Fabrication Division	3

All the questions were asked of interviewees at the branch manager level and above. A subset of the questions was asked of others. Each managerial interview took approximately 1 to 1½ hours. Other interviews took 20 to 30 minutes. As questions were being answered, both Mr. Kramm and I recorded answers or key points on blank copies of the interview schedule. The general topics covered by the interview schedule are shown in Figure 2. The responses serve as the basis for the Results and Implications sections of this report.

Figure 2 Topical coverage of interviews

1. Growth
   a. Sales dollars
   b. Personnel
   c. Types of business
   d. Business locations
   e. Data processing transaction level
2. DP resources and capability
   a. Computer hardware
      Capability
      Capacity
      Load
   b. Applications
      Types
      Committed modifications
   c. Personnel
      Numbers
      Skills
3. Managerial climate
   a. Systems satisfaction
      Current systems
      Current status
   b. Views toward computer as management tool
      Operations
      Control
      Decision making
   c. Attitudes about Management
      Centralization/decentralization
      Business integration/autonomy
   d. Attitudes on management of computer resource
      Equipment location
      Equipment selection
      Personnel location and reporting
      Charging

At the completion of each interview, each person was asked to complete a written, 1½-page Information Satisfaction Questionnaire and return it through the mail to Mr. Kramm. This questionnaire asked about satisfaction with the way the current information system provides certain categories of information and asked for an indication of how these categories ought to be provided.

In addition to the interviewing procedure other material covered in the next two sections of this report comes from interviews with Mr. Kramm and the corporation's data processing personnel. This material tends to be of a more factual nature and addresses hardware types and specifications, transaction volumes, and types of processing applications.

Results

This section will report the details of what we discovered about Perigee Industries as a result of the interviewing process. The implications of these findings for the data processing plan will be presented in the following major section of this report. The style to be used in reporting the results will be to list the major category and then, on a point-by-point basis, give the results. Occasionally, a comment of a more or less editorial nature will be made in the Results section.

Growth

1. Business volume, as measured by sales revenue, will about double in the next 5 years. Tulsa Manufacturing will have an especially high growth rate. Managers generally observed that, if anything, Perigee sales projections were slightly conservative.
2. Similarly, the number of total personnel in the corporation will just about double during the planning horizon.
3. According to "published" personnel growth projections, there will be no "divisional staff" 5 years hence. Further, projections are that the Perigee staff will grow from the present 13 to 20. Comment: I believe that the former will have to be rethought,

and that total staff projections are unrealistically low for a corporation of the size being forecast.

4. In terms of locations, substantial growth will occur at Thompson Mufflers, Thompson-Florida, a new branch, and Black Truck Installers.

5. Because of its uncertain nature at this time, we cannot take new types of business into account for data processing planning except to anticipate that the Branch Operations Division (BOD) may be engaged in some retail operations during the planning period.

6. Similarly, new business ventures, such as the new branch, are so vague that they will not have major implications for the data processing plan. Comment: Either a system will be acquired with a company or (perhaps preferably) processing can be provided by the system we are planning. The latter has some minor capacity or enhancement implications for the planned system.

7. Growth in the volume of transactions to be processed will occur at approximately the same rate as the growth in sales. This means that even with no new applications, the amount of transactions to be processed will substantially increase. If either a retail business or "deductible" insurance comes about within the BOD, the increase in transactions will be substantial. Comment: We have gathered data on transactions growth relative to sales for Thompson Mufflers an Plastacene-Texas, intending to do a correlational analysis and future projections. However, the day-to-day operational problems at both these locations have delayed data collection needed for the analysis. Although we do not have "good" data at this point, it is conservative to say that transactions growth can be projected as substantial. The growth at Thompson Mufflers will be especially rapid.

Data Processing Resources and Capability

1. The processing for the BOD is provided by the computer at Thompson Mufflers. This is an XYZ model

61/58, the smallest of the XYZ business computer line. The Thompson configuration, however, is at the top of the line. The hardware is capable of doing batch processing as well as online applications, but doing the latter stretches the system's capability. The central processor is relatively slow, and memory is limited. Fortunately for future applications, the programs are written in COBOL. There is no backup for the online applications; if the system is down, the warehouse's inventory system ceases to operate. Applications are primarily of a clerical/financial nature except for the online inventory system.

The system is fully loaded with the batch and online system operating. It is fair to say that about 80 hours per week are needed to process existing transaction levels. Thompson Mufflers has one capable programmer, a newly hired full-time operator, a part-time operator, and an experienced supervisor. There are severe reservations about the overall design of the Thompson Mufflers financial systems, in the sense that these systems appear to be extremely inefficient with regard to processing. Symptoms of the inadequate systems design are an inordinate amount of error-correction processing time and jobs not being able to be processed frequently enough.

2. The processing for the Plastacene-Texas branch of the Plastic Manufacturing Division (PMD) is also on an XYZ 61/58 computer. The configuration of this system, however, is at the minimum level. The same statements about the central processor made above apply here. Memory and storage are more limited in this system, and all applications programs are written in a subset of COBOL. Applications are of a financial nature, and a new production cost system is committed. At present, 40 hours per week are required to process the application programs.

The personnel status is hard to assess since a new programmer/analyst has just been hired to re-

place a programmer who left the company. The new
person has substantial experience, but is new to
Plastacene-Texas. Also present is one keypuncher/
operator and a part-time keypuncher. There is
no experienced data processing supervisor at
Plastacene-Texas.

3. At the Tulsa Manufacturing Branch of the PMD, there
   is an IBM PC/XT computer. This is a very small
   computer that is being used in job-cost estimation.
   This computer does not have the capability to perform business data processing in the volumes needed.
   Programs are being developed by the branch manager
   and controller. No business data processing is
   being done.

4. The only computer within the Austin Fabrication
   Division (AFD) is a ZOT/11 which is also used for
   job-cost estimation. The programs are being developed by an engineer and a college student hired for
   the summer. This computer could, with some enhancements and source software development or acquisition, be used for business data processing; but the
   language used would have to be BASIC, not COBOL. No
   business data processing is being done.

5. At other locations, Thompson-Florida and Plastacene-
   Louisiana, data processing services are being purchased on a limited basis from service bureaus.

6. The cost of data processing at Perigee is estimated
   in Figure 3.

This cost is approximately 0.6 percent of sales.
Personnel costs represent about half this amount.
Management has been informed by the consultant that an
average industry figure is 1 to 1.25 percent of sales
for data processing costs, with personnel expenses
accounting for twice as much as the computer equipment
expense. Comment: Naturally, in the case of Perigee
Industries, the expenses are divided very unequally
among the units. Thompson Mufflers is spending 1.3
percent of sales on data processing; whereas, in the
same division, Black Truck installers is spending virtually nothing.

**Figure 3 Current corporate data processing expendi-
tures.**

	Expenditures	Percentage of sales
Perigee staff	$ 30,000	
Branch Operating Divisions		
Thompson Mufflers	$ 90,000	
Thompson-Florida	12,000	
Parts Warehouse	9,500	
Jackrabbit Motors	1,200	
	112,700	0.62
Plastic Manufacturing Divisions		
Plastacene-Texas	$ 40,000	
Plastacene-Louisiana	600	
Tulsa Manufacturing	2,800	
	43,400	0.30
Austin Fabrication Division	38,000	0.45
Total	$224,100	0.58

Managerial Climate

1. Systems satisfaction. We took two measures of satisfaction with the data processing/information systems within the organization. One was an open-ended
   question evaluating the present state of affairs,
   problem areas, and areas of high satisfaction or
   success.   The other measure was the written questionnaire we left with each person interviewed.
   Figure 4 is a summary of the questionnaire results.
      As can be seen, there is a feeling that in all
   areas there is room for improvement in how systems
   can be used.   The largest gaps in present use as
   contrasted with desired use are at the top of the

figure.   Note that present systems are most useful
for saving time and reducing clerical costs, two
areas of high desired use.   The planning and budgeting areas are also areas of high desired systems
use, but at present the system is not too useful for
these activities.   Comment: Note that the figure
shows overall response.   The response from unit to
unit varies substantially.

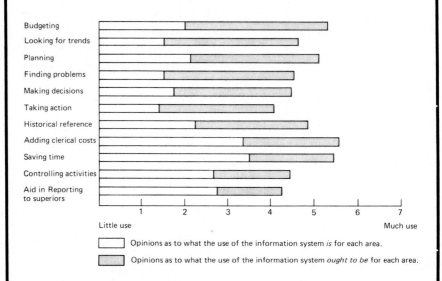

**Figure 4 Overall results of response to information
satisfaction questionnaire.**

The interview results are basically consistent
with the questionnaire findings.   Almost everyone
says what is present is good, but expresses a desire
to move ahead to do more.   This desire is especially
present in those locations that are not too far
along.   Thompson Mufflers, the most well developed,
tends to focus on problems with operational issues,
e.g., the need to get reports out on a more timely
basis.   Others want new systems developed (Plastacene) or a start on IS/DP development (Austin, Tulsa
Manufacturing).   Almost all want to move ahead with
a substantial resource commitment, but in an evolutionary, controlled manner.   Not one respondent
wanted to simply maintain the status quo.   Comment:

The desire for moving ahead with data processing development is substantially greater at the subordinate manager level than it is at the branch level and above. As a matter of fact, several personnel at the operating level appear to be "chafing at the bit" to get going, especially in the production area.

2. <u>View toward computers as a management tool</u>. Figure 4 and the answers to questions regarding future applications areas provide some clues as to how Perigee managers view the computer as a management tool. Basically, these persons want the computer to aid at the operational level and are not yet too concerned about the computer as an aid to decision making. Somewhat surprisingly, the use of information systems as a management control tool is not as highly regarded as one might expect. In essence, the nuts and bolts applications are more in demand. There is evidence at the Perigee level, however, that this is not so much the case. Here, utility is seen for control-oriented information systems as well as for planning systems. One branch, Plastacene-Texas, indicates a desire at all levels to make major applications expansion in the next 1 to 2 years. The production area is the prime consideration.

3. <u>Attitudes on business integration/autonomy</u>. There is a clear view here that there is little need for integration of components of the Perigee Corporation.

4. <u>Attitudes on business centralization/decentralization</u>. This is a vague area. The branch managers clearly want to be very decentralized and autonomous. They see Perigee as involved primarily in aggregate planning, acquisition decision making, and capital-raising activities. All other decisions should be made at local levels, according to branch managers. The view of what the division level should do is very vague and is defined differently according to each respondent. Comment: Partly because of the newness of the divisional concept, the views as to what the divisions ought to do depend on whom you ask. Over the coming years, the definition of the role of the division will be sharpened. One major problem is that in many cases at present the

differentiation between a division and a branch is not at all clear.

5. <u>Attitudes on management of the computer resource.</u> We asked several questions about who, in the corporation, should make decisions concerning: (1) location of equipment and types of equipment, (2) location of personnel, and (3) charging mechanisms for the computer. Presenting the results is difficult at best. In the first place, many of the decisions had implications the respondents clearly did not understand. Also, there were technical problems. For example, we got the feeling that most people thought that if two similar applications, say, accounts receivable, were processed on a central computer, they would have to be identical applications.

Another problem concerns the location of the ultimate decision authority. In general, people responded that the Perigee staff, being more expert, ought to make these decisions. However, when we pressed, we found out that the branch managers didn't really mean this. What they meant was that as long as there was no conflict, then Perigee staff should decide. Although they would not come right out and say it (very often), the impression came through strongly that branch managers feel that they have ultimate veto power.

One area we can comment upon is that of charging. Almost every respondent resisted the notion that the computer resource be provided free by the corporation or by a division. Yet, Mr. Kramm of the Perigee staff would at least consider the charging option as having some merit and not deserving of exclusion from our planning alternatives.

Implications

This section relates the implications that the preceding results of the survey have for the data processing plan. In this section, a number of conclusions will be drawn and opinions offered. The same section titles will be used here, and the style will parallel that of the previous section.

Growth

1. Even given no new applications, the existing computer systems are inadequate to handle projected transaction volume. Plastacene-Texas might be able to process existing applications throughout the planning horizon on a three-shift operation. Even this option (three shifts) will not suffice for Thompson Mufflers.
2. An absolute increase in personnel has no direct impact on the data processing plan other than that it reinforces the above conclusion.
3. Locational expansion, because of its nature and uncertainty, will not have a major impact on the plan. New businesses and possible retail trade will be kept in mind concerning the expandability of alternative systems.

Data Processing Resources and Capability

1. The Thompson Mufflers system is "stretched" to handle the existing applications and load. Action must be taken in the short term (6 months to 1 year) here. The Thompson Mufflers system is not expandable as is (without a substantial system upgrade). A high-priority application is a redesign of existing applications to make them efficient.
2. The Plastacene-Texas system is fully loaded as is. Second-shift operation may accommodate transaction growth, but managerial plans suggest a system upgrade in the intermediate future (1 to 3 years).
3. The systems at Austin Fabrication and Tulsa Manufacturing are not likely to be appropriate for general business data processing (especially for Tulsa Manufacturing). This fact suggests that if business applications are to be developed, new processing capability must be provided.
4. Existing systems are very vulnerable to the thinness in personnel. Plastacene-Texas' and Thompson Mufflers' recent experiences are examples. It should not be necessary for supervisory personnel or Perigee staff to work 6 days per week at 18 hours per day to solve this problem. System plans should provide buffers against the limited personnel problem.

5. New applications and/or systems redesign is severely hampered by lack of systems analyst skills in the corporation. Corporate management should consider the implications of what losing the one person with systems analysis skills would have for new systems development and even for the smooth functioning of the present system. The disruptions caused by turn-over in staff is a very key point I want to empha-size for management's attention.

6. As the data processing system grows in size and complexity, there will be a need for more managerial effort (planning, control) at the Perigee level.

7. It is not unrealistic to expect that total annual corporate data processing costs may rise to the $500,000 to $750,000 level by the end of the plan-ning period to support what its management want to do with the computer and to do so efficiently and effectively.

<u>Managerial climate</u>

1. The systems satisfaction measures indicate that there is a long way to go to create a completely satisfactory information system. At Thompson Muff-lers, the desire is for more efficiency and control-led growth. Plastacene-Texas would like a major information system with emphasis on production applications. At Tulsa Manufacturing and Austin Fabrication, the operational managers want pro-duction-oriented systems. The fact that the top management of these branches is somewhat less enthu-siastic and not presently ready to commit resources suggests applications development in a longer-run time frame.

2. We should not overlook the development of a few corporate-level systems in the short-run plan, e.g., a financial planning system.

3. Any applications growth, however, will be evolution-ary as contrasted with revolutionary.

4. Systems will be primarily operational in nature (with emphasis on time saving, clerical saving, production cost reduction). In manufacturing units,

production/inventory applications are in high demand.

5. There is no managerial need for systems integration across units.

6. Local units (branches) have expressed a strong desire for physical access to a computer facility. This means that branches should have either stand-alone computers connected to a central computer or remote-terminal access to a central computer.

7. The systems plan ought to provide some backup to the problems of limited personnel at the branch level.

8. If possible, some method ought to be found in the plan to protect against units being unable to operate when their computer is down (the online systems case).

9. Before a data processing plan is implemented, the Perigee corporate management must take responsibility for resolving the issue of where key decisions are to be made and develop a system for handling decisions regarding systems management decision making.

FUTURE DIRECTIONS

To complete this stage of the project, I will ask the management of Perigee Industries to react to this report. I would like to establish areas of agreement and disagreement. With regard to the latter, I would like to enter into a process by which we can isolate differences of opinion and either resolve these or at least agree that the differences must be taken into account in the planning process.

The next step of the project, Phase II, will be to develop an applications plan for the various Perigee units. The plan will list application areas for the computer by unit. Priorities and a time schedule will be given. Actually, substantial progress has been made in the identification of applications during the interviewing stage, so progress should be rapid. I would estimate that the applications plan will be developed by middle to late August.

ASSIGNMENT

1. Write a report which evaluates the interview result conclusions drawn by the consultant. In your report, make your own assessment of what these findings mean for the shape the ultimate data processing plan will take. Be specific on the latter, and make some preliminary judgments about equipment and staff placement and the nature of the ideal data processing configuration for the units of Perigee Industries. Be sure to relate your opinion to the information you have at this point.

2. Critique the interviewing process. In other words, do you agree with what was asked and the procedure used? If you find weaknesses, state what you would have done differently, and why.

As the consultant's phase I report to Perigee Industries as part of the 5-year data processing plan was being finalized, typed, and edited, several events at Thompson Mufflers had a dramatic impact upon the overall planning study. First, in late June, while the warehouse online system was being installed, the full-time operator gave notice and subsequently left the company. Then, the keypunch operator was fired and replaced by temporary personnel.

Next, in mid-July, on one of the hottest days of the summer in Dallas, Thompson Mufflers' air conditioning failed, causing the room temperature in the computer area to rise to over 100 degrees. The computer failed because of the heat. The computer vendor's maintenance personnel repaired the computer, but for the next month and a half, machine downtime was excessive. Sometimes, the machine was down more than 20 hours per week.

Even more severe was the fact that, on occasion, the machine failure occurred in the disk controller, causing master files to be destroyed. Roger Kramm was able to recreate these files from history files, but the computer time to do so sometimes took the better part of a weekend. While the system was down the warehouse transactions could not be entered; thus it was constantly necessary to work overtime when the system was available to catch up on warehouse transactions. Further complicating the situation in July was the fact that Thompson's programmer was on vacation for 3 weeks to attend a world championship track meet being held in Helsinki, Finland.

By August, matters had improved somewhat, so Roger Kramm and the consultant took time to attend a meeting at XYZ Computer Corp. (2 full days) to examine in detail the XYZ 62/40, the equipment that might replace the XYZ 61/58. Both were disturbed by what they learned. Although the equipment appeared powerful and would provide growth potential upward within the XYZ line, several major problems were detected.

It was learned that the level 62 computer series was designed to capture IBM system 34 customers and that it would be much easier to convert from an IBM system 34 to an XYZ level 62 than it would be to convert from an XYZ 61/58 to an XYZ 62/40. Not only would all programs presently running on the 61/58 in mini-COBOL have to be rewritten to full COBOL, but all files on the 61/58 would have to be converted to the 62/40 format. The latter would be extremely diffi-cult since no machine/machine conversion mechanism existed.

Thus, in mid-August, the situation was:

The Thompson Mufflers XYZ 61/58 was being operated on a third shift just to handle the current level of transac-tions.

A major systems redesign was needed at Thompson Mufflers to improve the work flow and processing. To simply install a faster computer would not significantly improve matters unless the systems flow was to be improved.

A major conversion effort would be required at Thompson Mufflers to upgrade to any new equipment.

At this time, the management at Thompson Mufflers was concerned because, with their difficulties plus the ware-house operating, they were not getting satisfactory perfor-mance in batch processing from their computer. They began to pressure the management of the Branch Operations division to take the warehouse off the system and return it to manual processing.

Roger Kramm and the consultant had, in mid-August, com-pleted an analysis of the processing volume at Thompson Mufflers. By examining fixed processing commitments, the effect of the systems degradation caused by the warehouse online system, downtime, and business-volume-related activ-ity, they prepared Figures 1 and 2. Figure 1 shows that, with the warehouse online, the Thompson Mufflers XYZ 61/58 must process into a third shift each day just to handle present business activity. Note that the short first shift (3.2 hours per day) shows the impact of the online system. Also, no time is shown for compilation associated with program maintenance or redesigned systems. Figure 2 shows what would happen if the warehouse system was removed.

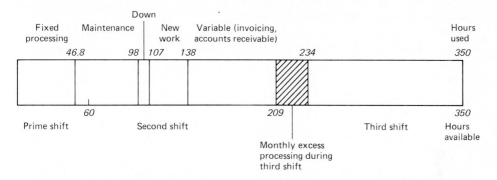

Figure 1 Monthly work load at Thompson Mufflers (warehouse online).

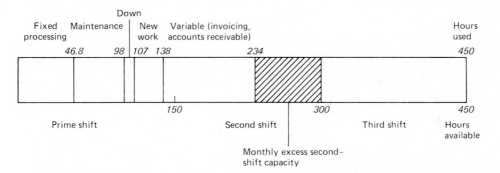

Figure 2 Monthly work load at Thompson Mufflers (warehouse offline).

It became very apparent to Kramm and the consultant that the Thompson Mufflers crisis had to be solved before they could talk about an applications plan. After all, when existing business volume is consuming all the available computer capacity and adding capacity is not possible without a major (and time-consuming) effort, it hardly makes sense to talk of new uses.

In late August, the Thompson Mufflers programmer gave notice that she would leave to take a position with another company. Early September was spent trying to develop a solution to the Thompson Mufflers problem that would be consistent with how the 5-year plan might develop. The phase II report was written, typed, and distributed to Perigee management in early October. As will be seen, the phase II report is quite different from what was originally planned. Only the last few pages of the report deal with an applications plan; most of the report addresses solving the very critical short-run problems and still being consistent with the form a longer-run plan might take.

REPORT TO PERIGEE INDUSTRIES
by
Systems Counsel
Phase II Report
(2 of 3)
October 4, 1982

MANAGEMENT SUMMARY

This report attempts to convince the management of Perigee Industries that a crisis situation exists in its data processing system. It is argued that a plan for future applications is infeasible until the current difficulties are resolved. The report presents a specific recommendation to overcome the short-run problem in an effective manner. In particular, the report recommends:

1. Hiring another systems analyst and programmer to assist in a conversion process
2. Upgrading the XYZ 61/58 system at Plastacene–Texas
3. If possible, installing a duplicate 61/58 system at Thompson Mufflers
4. Converting to new computer systems by approximately January 1984

A plan is detailed as to how to be ready to convert to the new system, and future applications for the new system are listed.

Overview of Phase II Report

As you will recall, our study of a 5-year data processing/information systems plan for Perigee Industries involves three phases. These are: (1) an examination of Perigee's current DP environment and managerial climate; (2) a plan for how the computer(s) will be used in the next 5-year period; and (3) a coupling of the organizational environment and the applications plan to form a projection of equipment and personnel needs over the planning horizon, plus a budget for the time period. This report addresses Phase II, the applications plan.

In this report, I will present a 5-year data processing applications plan. However, I will not do it with the completeness and degree of detail that was presented in the project proposal. The reason for the change is that recent events make the development of a detailed 5-year applications plan an exercise in futility, especially in the more distant years. Thus, in this report, I will concentrate on how Perigee Industries ought to evolve to the point where a multiyear projection of computer applications is meaningful.

As implied in the preceding paragraph, the study team has concluded that conditions in the current Perigee Industries data processing system are so serious that they must be improved before a serious future applications plan can be nontrivial. In a nutshell, there is no future for Perigee DP applications unless short-run ((2-year) steps are taken. I have concluded that to speak of new computer applications is virtually meaningless since existing conditions will preclude their development. These conditions are: (1) not enough computer capability and capacity, and (2) not enough people with time to develop new applications even if the proper computer hardware existed. Summarizing my position, there is no need for an applications plan because, unless steps are taken, Perigee Industries in the next 5 years will not be able to support even its existing DP applications, let alone consider new ones.

Having painted such a gloomy picture, I will, in the remainder of this report, suggest how we can improve the situation described above and then discuss future applications once their development becomes feasible. Thus, the applications plan will be divided into two parts: (1) a plan for preconversion and (2) a postconversion applications plan. From the previous sentence, the reader has undoubtedly become aware that I am suggesting that at some time in the next 5 years it will be necessary to upgrade Perigee's data processing hardware, i.e., conversion. Much of the discussion which follows will attempt to justify the need for conversion and to detail the steps required to convert.

The plan which follows and its justification stem from conditions described in the phase I report and events which have transpired since the submission of that report (July 26, 1982). Therefore, to begin my arguments, I would like to refer back to that report and to draw upon the subsequent relevant happenings.

A Reassessment of the Situation

In the phase I report, reference was made to the fact that both of the two major Perigee Industries computer centers were overloaded. Because of short-run problems at these centers in late June and early July, it was inappropriate to gather the data required to measure the load and to forecast future work loads. A promise was made in the phase I report to present this material at a later date.

Thompson Mufflers

When the analysis was performed, the hypotheses were confirmed. Figure 1 shows in detail the situation at Thompson Mufflers.

This figure shows that, with the warehouse online, 138 hours per month are used up by processing existing applications whose time is not a function of the level of business activity. In addition, 96 hours are occupied by volume-related activity (invoicing/accounts receivable).* The net result is that 25 of the processing hours must be done during the third shift. These figures are based on an estimate of 9 hours per month down because of machine failure and routine maintenance. Actual downtime experienced this summer plus the processing required for recovery has been roughly 3 times this amount.

*June activity of approximately 6000 invoices. It happens that this transactions volume is just about at the level of a 5-month average.

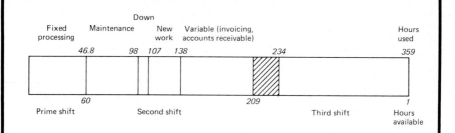

Figure 1 First shift shortened by effect of ware-house system.

Further complicating the situation is the fact that Thompson Mufflers has suffered an incredible 100 per-cent turnover in data processing personnel during the summer, and while all this was transpiring, brought up an online system to service the warehouse. I would now, based upon the facts at hand, describe the state of affairs at Thompson Mufflers as being much more critical than presented in the phase 1 report. Here you have an obsolete piece of computer equipment fully loaded by present transaction volumes, no programmer after October 1, in a location with a questionable power source, and the physical movement of the equip-ment scheduled in the near future.

Making matters worse is the fact that the system is not upgradable to more powerful equipment without a substantial reprogramming effort and file conversion. In addition, the design of the system (the way proces-sing takes place) is such that, in my opinion, a major systems redesign is required before new computer equip-ment of any kind can be effectively utilized. To bring in new hardware and simply convert existing programs would be like putting jet engines on the Kitty Hawk biplane.

Finally, it should be noted that the above scenario describes the current situation. If business volume grows, matters will become even worse as the number of transactions increase. Right now, we expect about 1.2

hours per day (on the average) is required of a third-shift operation. If sales grow by 10 percent, you will be up to 2 hours per day into a third-shift operation.

To let this situation continue is to be penny wise and pound foolish. There will come a point where, because of machine failure, personnel unavailability, or business growth, the system will not be able to keep up with transactions volumes and will get further and further behind. To avoid this situation and avoid consequences that are potentially harmful to the business health of Thompson Mufflers, action must be taken.

Plastacene-Texas

The situation in Denton is better than that at Thompson Mufflers, but is coming dangerously close to a position of remarkable similarity. The major difference is that with a modest upgrade of the XYZ 61/58 system at Plastacene-Texas, greater machine capacity can be obtained and a crisis situation delayed. Recall that the 61/58 at Thompson Mufflers is not further expandable, so to increase capacity, an upgrade to more powerful equipment is required.

Our study of the use of the computer at Plastacene-Texas shows that the computer is being utilized 105 hours per month for processing independent of business activity level and about 138 hours per month for transactions which vary with the activity level. In other words, the computer is busy about 55 hours per week or runs about 3 hours per day into a second shift. Similar to the Thompson Mufflers situation, Plastacene-Texas has (or will have) experienced 100 percent turnover in its data processing staff since our study began.

Somewhat complicating the Plastacene-Texas situation is the fact that, whereas Thompson Mufflers is considering reduction in its current applications of the computer, Plastacene-Texas has new applications planned. Keeping in mind that their systems analyst/programmer probably has to operate the computer about 16 hours per week, the applications growth will strain both the hardware system and the personnel situation. Further complicating matters at Plastacene-Texas is the fact that before the computer system can be upgraded to new equipment, all programs must be converted to full

COBOL. Any reprogramming will further strain the limited time availability of the hardware and personnel. Before COBOL conversions can take place, however, the present XYZ/58 system must be enhanced.

Having seen what has happened at Thompson Mufflers—it must convert equipment to handle the transactions volume; it must reprogram to full COBOL before it can convert to new equipment; and it can't reprogram to full COBOL because it doesn't have the processing time, given existing transactions—we must plan for Plastacene-Texas to be able to convert without this Catch-22 situation.

Implications for the Five-Year Applications Plan

While we were trying to develop the 5-year applications plan our analysis plus the events at Thompson Mufflers, as well as the somewhat immediately less-serious state of Plastacene-Texas, made us realize that to talk in terms of an ambitious 5-year application plan is folly. This condition was brought home by the fact that we were talking out of both sides of our mouths at the same time. On the one side we were considering inventory control applications; on the other, we were exploring shutting down the warehouse inventory system.

Thus, as matters now stand, I am persuaded that consideration of new applications for Thompson Mufflers and Plastacene-Texas* are nothing more than unachievable wishes. Further, because the situation is so critical at these major Perigee DP centers, potential profitable applications at Tulsa Manufacturing and Austin Fabrication will have to either wait or be instituted in an ad hoc manner by those managements as they desire. The difficulty of the latter procedure, of course, is that in the future they too may repeat the mistakes of the past, such that DP activity at Perigee Industries will continue on a crisis basis.

Viewing these conditions, I have concluded that there is only one viable applications plan for Perigee Industries, one that can be described as preconversion and postconversion. This plan is the subject of the remainder of this report.

*Beyond the commitments already made for general ledger, inventory flow accounting, and product costing.

Desired Future

It is our goal that in the 18- to 24-month time frame that Perigee Industries be in a position to implement computer applications that will assist its management in more profitably operating the organization and its subcomponents. At that time we want to have new equipment installed at Thompson Mufflers and be close to upgrading the processing capability at Plastacene-Texas. It is at this point that we can begin the new applications which will be listed shortly. Additionally, we would at least have the capability of also serving Austin Fabrication and/or Tulsa Manufacturing should the need arise. The question is, how do we get to this desired future?

Personnel

I hope that the reader has been convinced that prior to equipment conversion, COBOL program conversion is mandatory at both DP sites. An even more critical task is the systems redesign at Thompson Mufflers. These needs make it important that additional DP personnel be obtained to assist in the preconversion period.

Equipment

I trust that I have been clear on the point that new equipment before we are ready for it "systemwise" would be a mistake. We do, however, have to "buy time" at both DP locations to convert existing programs and compile modified new ones. I have four plans for doing this.

Plan 1. Obtain a duplicate 61/58 system for Thompson Mufflers. Upgrade Plastacene-Texas's 61/58 system.

Plan 2. If the vendor (XYZ) offers to install a new system (say, a 62/40) at an attractive price and will allow system conversion at Thompson and Plastacene-Texas to be spread over a proper time period, offload the warehouse onto such a system, put the system in a new location, and gradually convert over the Thompson batch system. Upgrade Plastacene 61/58 system.

Plan 3. Upgrade only the Plastacene-Texas 61/58 system.

Plan 4. Go back to manual at the warehouse, and return the Thompson Mufflers system to the batch system it had before the warehouse was placed online. Leave the Plastacene-Texas system as is and upgrade it some time in the future.

Plan 1 is clearly more desirable from our view. This is because it lets us do everything we are now doing, relieves the pressure of growing processing requirements from increasing business, and allows us to start program conversion. This plan, however, may be infeasible because of the vendor response to our request for a duplicate 61/58 at a reasonable cost or because Perigee management may reject such a system at the cost proposed by the vendor.

Plan 2 is hard to assess without knowing how attractive a deal will be offered. If much conversion assistance is offered for both the warehouse programs (initially) and, later, for the revised Thompson Mufflers systems, coupled with a very low price, then this alternative could be attractive. I would suggest, however, that a 1-year lease arrangement be considered to minimize the risk should the system prove unsatisfactory. With such protection, little time would be lost, and future flexibility would be maintained.

Plan 3 is clearly less desirable from a DP perspective. Under this plan, all programs (even Thompson Mufflers) would be compiled and debugged at Denton. The logistics of this operation alone make it undesirable, but feasible. Under such a plan, we might not have to return the parts warehouse to manual processing. Any substantial equipment failures or business-volume growth, however, would jeopardize the continued warehouse computer processing. This plan is feasible, but awkward and risky.

Plan 4 is disastrous in my view. It is a full retreat away from the solution of Perigee's present problems. Undoubtedly, this would be the lowest-cost short-run action but, in the long run, might be the most costly action Perigee Industries will ever take in data processing. In my opinion, this action would seriously jeopardize Perigee's long-run data processing future and would represent a failure by executive-level Perigee management to deal with a problem that is managerial and has little to do with technical or economic issues.

I would like Perigee management to think in terms of a major new computer system being operational in the January–May 1984 time period. Furthermore, I would suggest that support be given to the personnel and equipment expenses necessary to have new equipment by that time. To clarify, I am not ready at this time to say that the new equipment will support (at a minimum) both the Branch Operations division and the Plastic Manufacturing division or whether the new equipment will support only the former with the latter getting new equipment at a slightly later date. A firm recommendation on this issue will be presented in Phase III of the report.

The proposed timetable is:

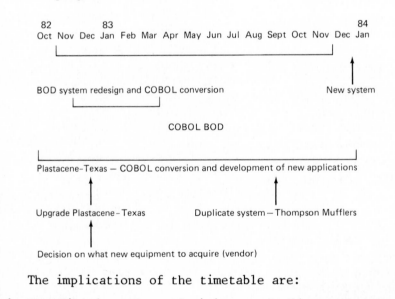

The implications of the timetable are:

1. Immediately make a decision to duplicate Thompson Mufflers' 61/58.
2. By November upgrade Plastacene-Texas computer.
3. By November begin COBOL conversions.
4. By March–April 1983, select vendor for new system.
5. By January–May 1984, install new systems and begin new applications.

RECOMMENDATION

It is my recommendation that to accomplish the above, Perigee:

1. Hire a systems analyst/programmer for the systems staff to do the COBOL conversion and assist in the Thompson Mufflers systems redesign.
2. Hire a programmer to maintain the Thompson Mufflers system while doing the systems redesign.
3. Upgrade the Plastacene-Texas 61/58 to a level capable of supporting full COBOL.
4. If XYZ will provide a duplicate 61/58 for Thompson Mufflers at anything near a reasonable cost, obtain such a system for a winter installation.
5. If a 62/40 warehouse system is proposed and is economically and managerially sound, obtain such a system for winter installation.
6. Avoid shutting down the system at the parts warehouse if at all feasible.
7. Appoint a Perigee executive to take charge of the data processing system and give this person the responsibility for the system and the authority to carry out its development.
8. If, because of the inadequacy of the vendor proposal or because of Perigee management decisions, plan 3 or plan 4 is adopted, it is suggested that phase III of this project not be undertaken. In the case of plan 3 being adopted, the money could better be spent on assistance in redesigning the Thompson Mufflers system. If plan 4 is adopted, there is no need for a systems equipment plan at this time.

SYSTEMS PLAN

Having spent a great deal of time on the arguments for systems conversion and how to achieve it, I now turn to my original goal, the presentation of an applications plan. The reader should keep in mind that I am now speaking of a development beginning probably in the fall of 1984. Thus, in terms of the original 5-year planning horizon:

83 Feb	84 Feb	85 Feb	86 Feb	87 Feb	88 Feb

Year 1	Year 2	Year 3	Year 4	Year 5

System conversion   New applications

Because the future is so uncertain, considering the conversion plus changing business conditions and management attitudes, I will only list the kinds of applications we foresee. Their planning and priority can be set in the later stages of systems conversion. As the hardware system is planned, it will be configured to support the following applications:

Corporate
 Financial planning
 Asset evaluation
 Financial statement consolidation
Branch Operations Division
 Financial planning
Thompson Mufflers
 Shop inventory management
 Insurance billing
Black Truck Installers
 Inventory management
 Costing/billing
 Sales analysis
Jackrabbit Motors
 Shop inventory management
 Insurance billing
Parts Warehouse
 Forecasting
 Model stock
Thompson-Florida
 Shop inventory management
 Insurance billing
Plastic Manufacturing Division
 Inventory control
 Job costing/bidding
 Backlog report enhancement
 Profit-and-Loss statement (weekly)

Sales analysis (production analysis, profitablity analysis)
Materials requirements planning
Consignment inventory system
Plastacene-Louisiana
    Duplicate of some Plastacene-Texas systems
Tulsa Manufacturing
    Job estimating
    Job profitability measurement
    Order entry
    Production scheduling
    Product cost/sales analysis
    Job costing
    Inventory control
    Materials requirements planning
    General ledger
    Machine loading
    Quality control analysis
    Resource productivity analysis
    Purchasing
    Backing analysis
Austin Fabrication Division
    Inventory control
    Materials requirements planning
    Production control
    Sales analysis
    Job costing
    Operations costing
    Cutting-list preparation
    Backlog analysis
    Plant loading
    Basic accounting

The reader should note that the above list (which is not in priority order) is a lengthy one and represents the ideas and desires of Perigee's personnel. The list is a result of the study team's interviews and was not generated by the team itself. We think that the desire for computer support for operations and management is clearly indicated by the above responses. We hope to be in a position in a year and a half to begin to be responsive to these felt needs.

MANAGERIAL ROLE

Near the end of the phase I report, a few comments were made concerning the role Perigee management ought to play in the systems development process. We have received several favorable comments from managers on our statements concerning the need for clarification of responsibility. Again, I plead for decisions and establishment of responsibility to address the recommendations made in this report. If management simply lets the situation slide and fails to accept the responsibility for decision making, then the plans suggested in this report cannot be realized. A particularly key decision which must be quickly faced is the recommendation regarding personnel. If you do not begin getting ready for conversion now, events could delay matters to the point where a start from scratch would have to be attempted at some future date to provide a data processing system for Perigee Industries.

LOOKING FORWARD TO THE PHASE III REPORT

Assuming that Perigee management reacts favorably to this report and its proposals, we will begin activity on phase III. This phase will concentrate on a detailed exploration of equipment options and personnel requirements over the 5-year period. These will be translated into budgets. In particular, we will explore the advantages, disadvantages, and costs of alternative equipment configurations and organizational structures. A recommendation will be forthcoming on the preferred alternative.

ASSIGNMENT

1. The consultant, in this report, has recommended delaying a full 5-year data processing plan for Perigee Industries. He, instead, concentrates on the short-run problems that must first be solved and makes some recommendations for their solution. Write a report evaluating both the consultant's action and his detailed recommendations. If you see shortcomings in his recommendations, suggest how they should be modified.

INTRODUCTION

In November 1982, the consultant delivered the final part (Phase III) of his report to the management of Perigee Industries. This report was the promised long-range information systems plan for the holding company. In the introduction to the plan he said:

This is the third and final section of my report regarding a 5-year data processing plan for Perigee Industries. As you will recall, this final phase of the project is to deliver the 5-year plan, broken down into equipment, personnel, and budget. These outputs are derived from the two previous parts of this study. The first phase involved the study of Perigee's present computerization and an assessment of: (1) how the corporation is likely to use the computer in the future, (2) the attitudes of its management concerning computerization, and (3) the future of Perigee Industries regarding growth, business types, etc. The second phase of the project examined in more detail the actual applications that will be made of the computer by Perigee units, thus giving insights into the types of processing and volumes that may be expected in the future.

159

Since the project began late last April, a number of events have dramatically impacted the nature of this study as well as its outputs. In particular, the events at Thompson Mufflers this summer led to a focus on solving short-run problems in one unit of the company that will still allow a meaningful 5-year data processing plan to be developed.

Before going on to the plan itself, I would like to paraphrase a statement made in my project proposal to Perigee Industries:

The requirements of the 5-year data processing plan are that it:

Be effective in processing transactions to support business activity.

Provide the desired level of support for management decision making.

Be cost effective.

Be flexible/evolvable.

As will be seen in the following report, the plan which is described is a "default" plan, in the sense that certain very desirable alternatives were not feasible. The plan fits the first two conditions and, possibly, the fourth. The plan does not fit point three at all; it is not at all cost effective. This statement will be fully explained as the report continues.

THE PLAN

The consultant's plan first laid out theoretical alternatives for locating equipment and personnel. Centralized, partially distributed, and fully distributed forms were presented. For each form, a budget was included. The total costs for equipment, personnel (broken out by type), training, consulting, supplies, purchased software, and data communications (where used) were: (1) centralization = $725,000; (2) central development/decentralized operation = $666,000; and (3) complete decentralization = $983,000. These are annual costs of the final year (5th year) of the plan. Some components (salaries) were inflated during the

latter years.   The plan also featured certain hardware expansion over the planning horizon and equipment costs modified for improving cost/performance ratios.

ASSIGNMENT

1. Develop fully the detail behind the three options presented in the consultant's report. Specify, for each option,
the type of equipment and its approximate cost; the personnel by type, location, and cost; any data communications
costs; and all other cost categories. Present your plan as
the system would be in the fifth year. Be sure to document
your assumptions about inflation rates applied to salaries
from year 1 to 5, fringe benefit costs (take a percent of
direct salary), maintenance costs (take a percent of annual
equipment expenses). See if you come up with approximately
the same level of annual costs and/or the same cost ratios
between the various plans.

Rapid Rental Systems, Inc., is a division of a very large financial holding company. Rapid itself is broken into its Car Rental, Truck Rental, Leasing, and General Rental divisions. Overall, the company generates approximately $450 million in revenue per year.

On September 28, 1983, a meeting was held at Rapid's corporate headquarters in Phoenix to discuss the subject of information processing. The meeting was triggered by two factors. First, Tom Burkholder, the company's president, had just returned from a meeting sponsored by The Conference Board at which the subject of information systems had been discussed. In particular, the discussion had centered on information as a corporate asset and the necessity of making the proper level of investment in an enterprise's data processing function. The second factor was the level of discontent among Rapid's divisional managers regarding the perceived benefits of EDP services given the rapidly escalating costs of providing those services.

The attendees at the meeting were:

Tom Burkholder, Rapid Rental Systems president
George Thomas, corporate controller (top computer executive)
Kevin Farr, corporate VP of information services
Division controllers (4)
Division vice presidents (4)

The opening remarks were made by Mr. Burkholder. Among other things he said were, "At the Conference Board meeting there was not one chief executive who felt he had a good way of determining the level to which an organization ought to invest in EDP. I heard several methods described, but as far as I'm concerned, none of them were worth much. Some simply base next year's EDP budget on last year's. Others go out and try to find out what similar firms are spending as a percentage of revenue or assets. Still others go through some elaborate process of adding up all the funding requests to get a total for the "wish" list and then end up cutting this figure back to an amount that the management feels will fit into the overall corporate budget. Frankly, I think we must invest in our corporate computing, but I'm uncomfortable with how we decide what level to spend. Any ideas from you gentlemen?"

One of the division VPs, Roger Anderson of Truck Rental, interjected, "I agree. Our total DP expenses have been increasing at 15 percent per year for the past 5 years. Because we allocate these out to the divisions based upon computer use, my DP costs have been going up at this same rate. As a profit center, my costs are rising and my profits aren't. Pretty soon, I'm going to be losing money just because of these EDP costs. If DP cost increases continue for 2 more years, they will put my whole division in the red."

"I'm in total agreement," said Milton Jones from the leasing division, "but I've got even a greater concern. Here we are with corporate computing continuing to add more people and buy more equipment and software. I just think they're inefficient and, because of the DP cost-allocation mechanism, simply passing these inefficiencies on to the rest of us. I don't want to pay as much for DP as I'm paying now and you, Tom, are asking whether or not we are investing enough in DP? I say invest less, not more."

"Yeah," echoed the leasing division controller, "I hear how cheap computing equipment is getting, and all we get is bigger bills with the new equipment."

Finally, Ralph Thomas, the manager of the general rental division, who had the reputation as a real hard-headed businessperson spoke up. "Look, we've been dissatisfied for years with the level of business support we've been getting from data processing. Let's simply agree to hold the line for the next 5 years on total DP cost. If equipment is getting cheaper for a given level of performance, which we all have heard that it is, we can insist that DP simply get more productive than it is now. This way we hold our level of investment and avoid the issue that Tom raised for 5 years. If, at the end of that time DP is doing a better job and we're more satisfied, then we can consider increasing the absolute level of DP expenditure. Assuming that revenues continue to increase during that period, then our level of DP expense as a percentage of revenue will really go down and we'll look good."

At this point, the meeting turned to a general discussion of each unit's problems. While this was taking place, Kevin Farr whispered to George Thomas, "I guess that I'd better forget about making a budget request for a fourth-generation language to support end-user query and reporting unless I can cut back on the budget somewhere else which, because so many costs are fixed, I'm not sure I can do."

"We'll see," responded Thomas.

After all the divisional personnel had spoken, Tom Burkholder asked Farr for his views. Farr said, "As you all know, we've been working on this problem for years, yet we clearly haven't been successful. There are several factors that I can identify that are pushing up our costs. First, all the divisions and the corporation are adding new applications, and our business volume is way up. Both these factors keep our equipment costs and personnel expenses up. Second, we (as with all our industry) have had severe turnover in personnel. Thus, our productivity is down. Third, we've had to go through an operating systems conversion, and now we're looking at another one since MVS-X/A is coming down the road. The conversion has drawn down upon some of our best people and caused a systems disruption. Finally, we've gone heavily toward online systems, and our data communications costs are up."

"Yes," said Anderson, "but these are your problems which have become my problem."

"Hold it," interjected Burkholder. "We're getting no-where. I suggest that we ask George for his comments."

"Well, we've got a problem, but so do a lot of others," Thomas stated. "I think we're looking at this the wrong way. I'd like to go back to Tom's original ideas. I think we've got to get more business service out of our DP func-tion and have it be more productive. To do this, we may have to make some more investments in the short run. There are some new tools and procedures that can provide good user service, increase the efficiency of the systems development process, and lower the high cost of maintaining existing systems. But these tools cost money. I'd suggest that we do just the opposite of what was suggested and, for the next 3 years, increase our investment in DP. I'd like permission to buy some productivity and service aids, and let Kevin's people use them for 3 years and then reevaluate our attitude toward DP. To make it easier for you profit-center managers to swallow, I would like to see my incremental DP budget for the next 3 years carried as corporate overhead."

"Great, George," said Tom Burkholder cynically. "We're back to one of my original concerns if we accept your propo-sal, how much should the increment be each year. In other words, how much should we be spending for DP. It's clear to me now that we could go on like this for hours and end up just as frustrated as we are now. I suggest that we hire a consultant to work with us on determining the level of DP expenditure and how we should establish this amount. As a matter of fact, I'm going to have Kevin suggest someone and he (or she) will work with a committee consisting of George, Roger, and I to solve this problem."

As the meeting was breaking up, Ralph Thomas called Burkholder aside and said, "I personally am so frustrated by DP costs and poor service that I am going to take advantage of personal computers in _my_ division. I've just approved an order for 20 of the little rascals. Frankly, I don't much care what is decided about the DP budget because in a few years I think we'll be going our own way for most of our computing needs."

ASSIGNMENT

1. Give an assessment of this situation.
(a) Does it represent a common problem, and do you think the views are real?
(b) What is the problem here?
2. Suppose you are the consultant who is hired. What would you tell these managers about establishing their level of DP expenditure?
3. Would you give them any other advice?
4. What is the implication of the statement made by Mr. Thomas at the end of the meeting, and how does it affect the situation?

After the meeting in Phoenix to discuss the productivity of Rapid Rental's data processing organization and the level of resources devoted to organizational data processing, two of the divisional vice presidents, Roger Anderson (Truck) and Frank Stride (Leasing), got together for dinner at the airport prior to catching planes to their respective divisional locations. The conversation soon turned to the data processing cost/benefit problem. Anderson said, "Look, as far as I'm concerned, all the discussion in the world is useless until I have some way of accurately assessing a data processing project's benefits. Oh sure they can show me how much I can save in not having to hire additional people and because I can get better utilization on my fleet. But what about those intangibles? We're looking at developing a marketing information system at a cost of about $100,000. So what if I know what I'm renting, where, and to whom? Is this worth a hundred thousand bucks?"

ASSIGNMENT

1. How should project benefits, especially the intangibles, be treated? Can the project benefits be summed over all projects to come up with the overall benefit of the corporate EDP function? Does senior management have a role in dealing with these issues? If not, why not? If so, what?

BACKGROUND

Richard, Dennis & Lewis is a full-range, progressive law firm specializing in trial work. It has two offices, one in Milwaukee and the other in Waukesha, Wisconsin. There are 55 attorneys in the firm (split 40 and 15 between the two offices) and approximately 85 support staff (including paraprofessionals). Fee income for the last fiscal year approximated $8 million. The support services are highly mechanized with a heavy use of automatic typewriters, copiers, and interconnect (non-Bell) telephone systems in both offices.

The Milwaukee office has approximately 8000 active clients. All billings are prepared by secretaries without use of automation. The general ledger is prepared monthly on an office and on a combined basis. An annual, overall financial "projection" is prepared, but there is no formal reporting against it. The firm reports its income on a modified cash basis.

In the early 1970s, Harriet A. Olson, the managing partner, recognized the need to utilize automated data processing equipment to process the firm's time records. At that time she contracted with a small private service bureau (a one-person operation that rented time on various large com-

puters) to program and run a monthly balance-forward, time-
record system. This provided a monthly report of time for
each attorney and each staff member. The report showed time
spent this month and time spent year-to-date divided into
various categories of billable and nonbillable time. The
time reports had a fairly high rate of error because of
incorrect input and the time delay before the output could
be reviewed for accuracy. The firm's records for client
disbursements, accounts receivable, and general ledger
were maintained on a mechanical, magnetic-strip posting
machine.

The system of service bureau time reporting and posting
machine for other records was maintained for approximately
10 years, utilizing a number of different service bureau
companies, until the posting machine experienced an unacceptable hardware-based error rate and the firm was quoted a
large repair bill (with no assurance that the repairs would
solve the machine-error problems). Faced with the prospects
of having to invest in a new posting machine and maintaining
a time-recording system that was filled with inaccuracies,
Ms. Olson decided to explore the fledgling general-purpose,
business microcomputer market of the early 1980s, in an
effort to combine all the processing functions into an
integrated, in-house computer system.

THE SELECTION PROCESS

Early in 1982, Ms. Olson received permission from her part-
ners to pursue her search for a new in-house microcomputer.
Remembering all the horror stories she had heard and read
about data processing vendors, Ms. Olson decided to deal
only with a well-known firm (i.e., Interactive Byte Machine,
Baker Corporation, Universal Computers, and Nationwide Computer Resources).

The First Selection

The selection process was quickly narrowed to Interactive.
Serious negotiations and discussions were held late in 1982
in an attempt to identify both the software systems needs
and hardware configuration. Those conversations were taped,
with the knowledge of all parties, to facilitate documentation of the agreement. Computer Universe, a firm providing

software for Interactive Computers had met with the office manager, bookkeeper, and other "interested" individuals in the firm in order to define the content and volumes of both the present and projected systems.

Early in 1983, a purchase agreement was signed for an Interactive, personal computer, for delivery after June 30 of that year. The machine was to have 256 K of memory and 20 Mbytes of hard disk.

The executive committee of the law firm approved the action and everything went well until it came time for the 90-day commitment letter to be signed (i.e., the Computer Universe letter of agreement). After reading the fine print of the agreement carefully, as lawyers are wont to do, Ms. Olson determined that Computer Universe had effectively exempted itself from guaranteeing anything more than that the hardware would accomplish engineering specifications. Ms. Olson refused to sign the agreement until Computer Universe added a paragraph guaranteeing that the hardware would perform the functions outlined in her discussions with their salespeople. The third-party vendor steadfastly refused to alter its contract. This disagreement was carried to the president of Computer Universe. When this firm rejected an amendment of any kind to its contract, Ms. Olson rescinded her earlier commitment and began the search for a new vendor.

The Second Selection

Late in 1983, Ms. Olson, together with her office manager, Peter Kolm, began negotiating with a vendor called Systems Professionals, that proposed a system based upon Baker Corporation micros. Again tape recordings of all conversations were made. A copy of the tape that contained a description of the proposed system was then forwarded to the Systems Professionals headquarters, with an addendum to its standard contract stating, in effect, that Systems Professionals agreed to provide the capabilities outlined on the tape. In March 1984, a formal contract calling for a Baker 1980 system was signed and approved by the firm's executive committee. Systems Professionals was to provide all software support for the new system. The Baker system contained 128 K of memory, a 10 Mbyte hard disk, and a letter-quality printer.

INSTALLATION

Systems development plans were started immediately. In June 1984, Dr. Allen Wilson, a local "consultant"/programmer was hired by Systems Professionals to act as a consultant and to undertake the software development and programming portion of the contract. Software progress then halted, because Dr. Wilson did not have access to a Baker computer upon which to test his programs. Although the Baker 1800 microcomputer system had COBOL and database languages, Peter Kolm and Dr. Wilson decided that all programming for the firm's applications would be done in BASIC (also available on the Baker 1800), because Dr. Wilson was an excellent BASIC programmer.

The hardware was delivered in July. In August, a new administrator-controller, John Peterson, was hired. The lack of appropriate plans and documentation (particularly an implementation schedule) shocked him. Unfortunately, he immediately became bogged down in personnel matters and had little or no time to spend on the computer project. Another fateful decision was also made at this time by Wilson and Peterson. They decided not to parallel test the new systems. All efforts were to be put into the new systems development, instead of maintaining two systems. Olson reluctantly agreed with the decision.

THE DISASTER

The following is a brief synopsis of the major problems encountered over the first 9 months of the installation:

1. The operating system used on the Baker machine had an undetected bug in its sorting routines. It could sort files with hundreds of transactions but could not sort files with a dozen or less transactions. The first of six updated and improved versions of the operating system that the firm was to receive over the course of the next 12 months cured this problem.
2. As files were built and additional programs were written and tested, the capacity of the disk drive was quickly used up. A second 10 MB drive temporarily solved the

problem, but this was the maximum amount of secondary storage available on the system and its limit was quickly reached.

3. The new versions of the operating system required additional memory, so some programs were limited in the amount of data they could handle (an additional 128 K of memory was also added, but this was the system's limit).

4. The programming effort bogged down because there was:
   a. No overall, documented plan
   b. Lack of communication between Don Smith, the bookkeeper, and Wilson
   c. No program documentation
   d. Increasing disinterest in the project by Wilson as the project dragged on and on. (He was working with a fixed-price contract.)

   Even the addition of a new programmer, Roger Busch, to Wilson's staff, only solved the problem temporarily. This addition treated only the symptoms, not the causes, of the problems.

5. Because of all the delays, and the resulting frustration, Don Smith began to sabotage the project. He sulked, pouted, and in general refused to cooperate with anyone. Peterson tried to move him out of the project but was overridden by Olson because "he is the only one who knows what he wants in the final system."

6. The first payment under the terms of the contract was made on August 15, 1984, and on August 29, 1984 (2 weeks later), a disk drive malfunctioned. The problem was not diagnosed for 30 days, so the month of September was lost! (Needless to say, the September payment to Systems Professionals was not made.)

ASSIGNMENT

1. Assume you are a computer consultant hired by Olson. Evaluate the actions of the firm to date. Describe a plan of action that the firm should follow. Keep in mind the size of the firm and its fairly modest processing requirements.

Southcentral Co-op is a very large agricultural cooperative consisting of three major divisions: Agricultural Products, Milk and Ice Cream, and Cheese. Dallas is the co-op's headquarters as well as the location of the Milk and Ice Cream division. The largest and most profitable division is Agricultural Products, which is located in Tulsa, Oklahoma. The Cheese division is located in Fort Smith, Arkansas.

For the most part, the data processing services for all the divisions have been located at the headquarters of the cooperative. All computer operations and the development staff are located within the co-op's information systems department (ISD) and report to a vice president, Ralph Thompson. Each of the divisions has an information systems manager, who is responsible for communicating the information systems needs of the division to the centralized data processing unit. In addition, the divisional information systems managers form a committee (along with Ralph Thompson) that is advisory to the cooperative's chief information officer and controller, Peter Brown.

In November 1983, Brown wrote the memorandum which appears on the next page to Ralph Thompson. The individuals named in the memo are all information systems managers with the various divisions.

MEMO TO: Ralph Thompson
FROM: Peter Brown
SUBJECT: Control of Data Processing Expenses

This memo is a brief review of two management sessions held last week in which the above subject was discussed. The first session was an informal meeting attended by Ken Johnson, Bill Goodman, and myself, in which they wanted to share some concerns they and the Tulsa working committee have concerning data processing efficiency, control, and effectiveness.

1. Are we (Agricultural Products) efficient users of data processing?
2. What criteria should we use to determine whether we are efficient?
3. How do we (Dallas) control ISD expenditures (allocations)?
4. Are we getting our money's worth or return from these expenditures?

Ken also presented the following chart showing budgeted and actual allocations from Dallas to the Agricultural Products division for 1979 through budget 1983.

	Budget	Actual
1983	$789,000	N/A
1982	659,000	$791,000
1981	540,000	599,000
1980	339,000	377,000
1979	320,000	331,000

While he was not absolutely certain about the accuracy of the above figures, Ken used them to illustrate some of their concerns. For instance, what has caused the increase in the level of these allocations, and why are the actuals trending so far in excess of budget? I told Ken we would review the numbers and get back to them on each of these questions.

Concerning the four previous questions, the first dealt with our ability to be efficient users. For example, why was the feed project allowed to run online when the cost differential to batch processing was so great? Are the rates that we use to charge services reflective of the costs of those different services?   Should we have differential penalties?   Should we have an annual review of all projects to determine whether they are being run on the most efficient basis?

This gets us into the second question: efficiency measurement criteria.   Should we have criteria established that would dictate when items would be put on and taken off at high- or higher-priority times?   Do we document and cost-justify the selection of various service levels?

The third question, the control of ISD expenditures, relates to the previous table.   There was a feeling Agricultural Products has to do a beter job of monitoring the month-to-month allocations from Dallas.   No one in the Agricultural Products Operation currently has that responsibility, but it will be assigned to Jim Walters in the near future.   We, of course, will work closely with Jim in his new role.

The fourth question is one that we have addressed many times but have yet to come up with an acceptable solution. Ralph, I reviewed with Ken and Bill your work on intangible project benefits and per-unit operating cost measurement. We also discussed the need to identify the on-going services provided to the divisions and the cost of those services in terms of per-unit volume (per ton of feed, etc.).   We agreed that this latter item would add perspective in the evaluation of total costs.

In general, I feel the session with Ken and Bill was very beneficial, and I think they were able to verbalize some of their frustrations and perhaps give us some future direction.   I think we must:

1. Provide more or better monthly charge information.   It should relate to budget and be broken out by major areas of service.
2. Analyze the Agricultural Products division's figures and provide answers to the questions asked.
3. Address the question of why frustrations exist and the reasons they have not been discussed or resolved and, at a lower level, what stops us from working together?

4. Review our methods of allocating processing costs, including the differentials that are placed on various levels of service.
5. Continue to stress the importance of project cost/benefit relationships and processing costs on a unit measurement basis.
6. Address all the questions raised above, and provide thoughtful, positive, and constructive responses in the team spirit that we value so highly.

I offered to review our operating standards of performance, but they felt we were doing a good job of control and communication in that area.

The second session raised the issue of control of data processing expense on an impromptu basis during our strategic issues seminar. Although that issue was not directly addressed by our Tulsa people, the session included many of the same concerns that were discussed with Ken and Bill. Principal issues were: (1) how do we measure overall benefit of our data processing costs, and (2) how do we control these costs—both developmental and operational?

These questions were raised in a very positive way and were directed not only to data processing but also to R & D, advertising, etc. Our president reiterated his perspective of the need to manage with information and his feeling that we have a way to go in this area. Although he expects that costs will be incurred in the planning and development of this information, he stressed the importance of the review of current costs, i.e., analysis projects and operations that were not meaningful and not justifiable from a benefit basis.

I suspect from the intense interest in this discussion, that our data processing areas will receive much attention over the next few years. I feel we have a tremendous opportunity, through this attention, to contribute significantly to the overall management information and management process in Southcentral Co-op.

I would be interested in your thoughts regarding the above and the direction you think we should take in meeting this opportunity to contribute.

ASSIGNMENT

1. Write a memorandum from Ralph Thompson to Peter Brown which responds to Brown's request for thoughts on the questions and issues raised in his memorandum.

Southwestern Hospital is a medical center complex located in Phoenix. The center consists of a prestigious clinic and three satellite hospitals. Each hospital has the ability to support over 700 beds.

Patients from outside the Phoenix area generally come to Southwestern Clinic to have complicated medical problems diagnosed. Upon diagnosis, patients are generally assigned to one of the three hospitals while treatment is given. Local patients often go directly to the hospitals for routine problems and can be admitted directly.

Computing systems for Southwestern Hospital are situated at the clinic, with satellite minicomputers located at each of the satellite hospitals.

The information systems department is run by Ms. Mary Ward, who has been with Southwestern Hospital during her 12-year information systems career. She started as a systems analyst fresh out of an MBA program, and has worked her way up to the director of information systems.

The hospital has had reasonable success implementing basic applications in the financial and patient services and auxiliary services area. Its even had some success with a couple of decision support systems to help in the budgeting area.

During the past 5 years, end-user computing has become a major phenomenon. There are currently 250 personal computers located throughout the medical clinic and hospitals. With this proliferation, there has been increasing demand to support end-user computing, as many end-users have begun to develop their own systems.

Information systems is having some difficulty deciding how to respond to this service requirement. They have always been organized into two basic units—systems development and production. Systems development consists of analysts and programmers. Specific analysts are assigned major responsibilities, such as financial, personnel, or patient services. Programmers are then organized into a pool from which the analysts can draw to support their various projects.

Production consists of computer operations, order-entry, data-control, and technical services. Its primary responsibility is the production processing of all existing applications and handling any special enhancements or maintenance to the operating system through the technical services staff.

The end-users are continually calling and asking questions or asking programmers or analysts to assist them with programs that they're working on. Ward's staff has begun to complain that they simply don't have time to do their other duties and support the end-user projects. She also has complaints from the end-user managers that the information systems staff is not very cooperative and often gives them incorrect information when they are asking for assistance. Some of the users go so far as to suggest that the systems staff resents the end-users systems development and are, to a certain extent, going out of their way to ensure that those projects fail.

Ms. Ward attended a professional conference, during which the notion of an information center was proposed as a way to provide end-user services, such as consulting and education. The concept seems to be applicable to her situation, so during her next staff meeting with the head of systems development and head of production, she raises the issue. Both Mr. Norm Wismer, manager of information systems, and Ms. Margarite Childs, head of production, think it's an excellent idea. The only problem is they both feel they should have responsibility for it. Mr. Wismer feels that the information center should be in systems development, because it is basically to support end-user development. Ms. Childs, on the other hand, argues that the type of work is more consulting and specialized and is more compatible with the technical-services type of staff that she currently has. She further points out that the end-users have not been satisfied with the support they've been getting from systems development. Mr. Wismer disagrees. He doesn't think technical services should even be in operations. He feels that operations is primarily a production activity, that some of the more innovative types of things happen because of technical service's location, and that technical services and the information center would better be served under him.

Ms. Ward suggests the possibility of setting up the information center as a separate activity. Both Mr. Wismer and Ms. Childs respond negatively to that. They point out that there would be too many chiefs and not enough Indians. Besides it would be impossible, argues Mr. Wismer, to coordinate systems development if there is a separate activity trying to encourage user-developed systems, especially when end-users are getting into things they shouldn't be getting into as it is. Ms. Childs further argues that information centers should be helping users take advantage of their existing systems by using user-friendly languages to do ad hoc inquiries to existing databases. End-user computing, she feels, is most compatible with production.

ASSIGNMENT

1. How do you recommend Ms. Ward organize the information systems department to incorporate services for end-user computing?
2. Given the dynamics of the people involved, in what way should Ms. Ward implement her chosen strategy?

Superfoods is a national grocery wholesale and retail chain. It has both company-owned supermarkets, as well as franchises. Currently, 40 percent of the supermarkets are owned by Superfoods, and the remaining 60 percent are franchised (but owned separately from Superfoods). However, all supermarkets buy their grocery products directly from Superfoods. Annual sales of Superfoods exceed $1.8 billion.

A key dimension of Superfood's franchising ability has been its willingness to share the computer systems it uses to support its own stores with franchisees. This allows a rather small grocer to have access to large, sophisticated, point-of-sale-based systems to support sales processing and by-product inventory management. That is, the retail terminals use bar-coding technology to capture inventory as well as price information. This information is then used to provide financial sales analysis, as well as inventory management and direct ordering of stock replacement through Superfood's warehouse outlets.

Although the concept has been well-received in the marketplace, much of the software available on the retail terminals, store-level computers, and Superfood's central computer has been both error-prone and late in availability.

To address this problem, Mr. Norm Chervany, vice president of information systems, has brought in a new director of systems development, Ms. Lynn Gallegos. Ms. Gallegos has an excellent reputation in software management and often is asked to speak at local DPMA and ASM chapters on the concepts and techniques she uses to manage large software projects.

After arriving on the job and spending a couple of months assessing the situation, Ms. Gallegos realizes that the software development group is totally void of any quality assurance processes. She discusses concepts, such as design overviews, structured walkthroughs, and code inspections, as means of improving software development and also discusses the notions of <u>problem</u> and <u>change</u> management as ways to better manage enhancements or corrections to existing software.

Her staff rebels at the idea of quality assurance concepts and problem and change management. They argue that it's just that much more red tape and that it would interfere with their productivity.

Further investigation by Ms. Gallegos in evaluating the software developed at Superfoods indicates that though good software engineering principles are defined in the software development procedures to be used by systems developers, those principles are virtually ignored in the software that is developed.

Ms. Gallegos calls a staff meeting and reviews her perception of the problem with software development and the primary factor contributing to late and error-prone software. She explains that, to rectify the situation, software engineering principles will be enforced and that quality assurance procedures, including design overview, structured walkthroughs and code inspections, will be implemented.

The staff mumbles somewhat at the recommendation, but there are no direct arguments against her instructions.

Six months later, Ms. Gallegos observes that software is still late and they are still having the error problems. Upon further investigation, she discovers that the staff is collectively ignoring her instructions and not adhering to her quality assurance procedures. She has several one-on-one meetings with key staff people to discuss the problem. They politely respond that they are really just too busy to mess with that "nonsense." They would like to do what she wants, but they just don't have time with their busy schedules.

Ms. Gallegos calls another staff meeting and indicates that she is aware that people are not following the instructions to use software engineering concepts and adhere to quality assurance procedures. She explains that she is putting her foot down on this issue and expects compliance.

The following day, a group of the more veteran systems developers go over her head to the vice president of information systems development and complain that Ms. Gallegos is making a bad situation even worse with her unrealistic demands. Mr. Chervany asks Ms. Gallegos, at the next management meeting, why there is so much resistance to the software engineering and quality assurance procedures she's attempting to implement, particularly if they are such a good idea. He states he is all for improving software development activities, but not at the expense of creating a serious morale problem. He asks her to present the facts supporting what she's trying to implement so that he can review them and make a decision. He's not familiar with the concepts, but if they make sense to him, he will support her. If they don't make sense, then he's going to ask her to come up with a different strategy.

ASSIGNMENT

1. Prepare a memo outlining the advantages to good software engineering and quality assurance procedures that Ms. Gallegos could present to Mr. Chervany.
2. What else could Ms. Gallegos do to assist in implementing the procedures she is advocating?

Superior Stationery Products (SSP) is a company whose main business is selling stationery and stationery-related products on a national basis. The principal customers are department stores (the stationery departments), stationery stores, and discount stores. SSP also prints individual letterhead stationery on a very fast turnaround basis. This product, which has been very successful, can be ordered through the various stores. SSP is considering direct order of this type of stationery by mail or telephone order, based upon magazine advertisements, but has not yet committed to this market segment.

Counting all customers, small and large, Superior sells to over 11,000 outlets. In 1982, total sales amounted to $730 million. The salesforce calling on the customers (stores) numbers 90. Sales are managed by territory, zone, region, and nationally. The organization of the marketing department is shown on the next page. The salesforce reports through the VP of sales.

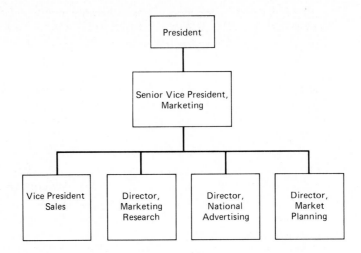

A constant concern of the senior marketing executives has been marketing information or the lack of same. The group constantly complained that a substantial amount of data existed but little information. As of 1982, several different reports were being produced by the firm's data processing department. The major reports are:

Sales analysis. A report for every customer Superior serves. Updated monthly, the report shows, by month and year to date, units sold and dollars sold for 66 products. Data is reported for current year and past year.

Consolidated customer history report. Information derived from the customer history and the sales analysis report. Updated quarterly, this report shows dollar sales by sales region and product type. It also depicts the number of each type of customer in each region (there are four basic types of customers and five major product families). Details also give a regional report by zone.

Monthly territorial report. Shows, by region, unit sales by major product category. Product categories do not match those used on the consolidated customer history report.

Sales report. Updated monthly, quarterly, and year to date. The report is also updated weekly (by state only). It shows units sold and dollars sold by all 66 products and is broken out by the plant that produced the product (there are six plants located around the country).

<u>Top fifty report</u>.   Updated quarterly on a manual basis. This shows, for the 50 largest customers, the customer name, city, sales dollars for this year and the past year.

The marketing department had budgeted for an information systems project and had been successful in getting this project into the data processing project list for 1983. The project is to completely redo all the current marketing information systems and to produce one system which will produce the proper information in the right time frame and do so accurately and consistently. All these properties are acknowledged to be missing with the old systems.

Problems quickly arose early in 1983 when the marketing department met to discuss how to organize for the information systems project. Mr. Rogers, the senior VP for marketing, simply wanted to turn the entire job over to data processing, even though DP had a history of not being responsive to user needs. His position is:

> Based upon DP's estimates, we've budgeted $125,000 during the coming year for development of a marketing information system. I certainly don't have the expertise to say what that is. We pay the DP analysts big bucks to be experts on information systems, so we should turn to them for the design of this system. I don't understand file sizes and computer hardware; I want to turn the job over to them.

Very quickly Mr. Harris, the director of market planning, expressed the completely opposite view:

> What you say is true; we're not computer experts, but we are supposedly experts in marketing. I've just been reading some material in the *Harvard Business Review* about "critical success factors," and I think we should isolate these for marketing. I suggest, as a matter of fact, that we ought to determine what the system is to do; that is, what should it produce? I believe that this is called "information requirements analysis." My suggestion is that we do a top-down design. I'd like to have the five of us form a team to do the basic design of the system. We can get a DP analyst to be a member of our task force to cover any technical issues.

Mr. From, the VP of sales, spoke up.

Wait a minute. There are several things wrong with what
you're suggesting. In the first place, designing information systems involves a great deal of technical knowledge that we don't have and can't get from one analyst.
It's not our job to build computer systems. This notion
relates to my second point, which is that I run a profit
center, sales. I don't get paid for or evaluated on my
ability to build information systems. Finally, I don't
know how much time is being suggested to do the design,
but whatever it is, I don't have it. My job is managing
sales, not screwing around with computers.

"How about a compromise?" suggested Mr. Jones, the director of marketing research. "Why don't we reverse the idea
of a task force? Why don't we put a marketing representative on the team of DP analysts?"
At this point, several minutes were spent discussing who
might serve as a representative. Mr. Harris insisted that
no one person would have a total perspective. Mr. Rogers
and Mr. From strongly urged that the person be an employee
from the planning group. Finally, Mr. Harris was asked if
he would be willing to serve, since he had the best total
perspective of anyone who seemed to be interested. When
pressed, he said, "I might be able to spend a few hours a
week on such a project, but I don't like this solution."
More discussion transpired until the following alternatives
were identified.

1. Turn the project over to DP with a written statement
   (about three pages at present) of what is required and let
   them build the system.
2. Do option 1 and appoint Roger Floyd, a recently hired
   member of the marketing planning group, to work full time
   with DP to make sure the proper system is developed.
3. Ask, instead, that Mr. Harris allocate a half day each
   week to work with DP on the project.
4. Ask each manager present to allocate 2 hours per week for
   the next month and a half to meet individually with DP
   and later to meet as a group for about 2 hours a week to
   go over what DP designs.

5. Bite the bullet and have each manager allocate 2 half days each week for a month to work with a DP representative to do the top-level design of the system. About 2 hours per week for the following 2 months would be required for meetings to review changes and progress.
6. Essentially use option 5, but use a representative from each rather than using the senior managers.
7. Institute option 5, except use three rather than five managers.
8. The same as option 7, except that the representatives would be as in option 6.

ASSIGNMENT

1. Evaluate the strengths and weaknesses of each alternative.
2. Which do you recommend?
(a) One of the above alternatives (no changes).
(b) One of the above alternatives, but with a variation (describe it).
(c) An alternative not listed (describe it).

Information Systems Incorporated (ISI) is a regional consulting firm located in Atlanta, Georgia. It specializes in information systems design, evaluation of organizational information systems departments and in systems planning. Frequently, it supplements its staff by using faculty from universities located in the Atlanta vicinity.

In the summer of 1983, a senior partner of ISI, Dr. John Garrison, received a telephone call from Mr. Thomas Davis of Superior Stationery Products, Inc. Superior Stationery is a well-known firm, of *Fortune*-1000 size, in the Atlanta business community. It had not previously used ISI's services, but had heard of the quality of ISI's work from other clients.

After a few initial remarks, Mr. Davis, who had identified himself as a staff analyst within Superior's newly formed market planning organization, got to the reason for his call. He asked, "Can you obtain a marketing information system for us?" Dr. Garrison was somewhat taken aback by the way the question was phrased. To him, the implication was that what was being requested was to direct Superior to an "off the shelf" marketing information system. After pursuing the issue a bit, Garrison understood that Davis believed that ISI could simply come in and detail for Superior the marketing information system that would be best for it.

Dr. Garrison knew very well that no such thing as *A* marketing information system existed. Thus, he suggested a meeting to discuss the matter further. In mid-July, Mr. Davis and Dr. Garrison met again. Each invited one other person. Mr. Davis brought along Mr. Harris, director of market planning for Superior. Dr. Garrison invited Professor Williamson, a member of a local university's marketing faculty.

At the meeting, the initial discussion concentrated on background information regarding Superior Stationery. Mr. Davis noted that the company's main business is selling stationery and stationery-related products on a national basis to department stores, stationery stores, and discount stores. He also provided data regarding company size and organization (given in Part A of this case).

Next, Mr. Davis and Mr. Harris both commented that much marketing data exists, but pointed out that it was not particularly useful. Davis then described the nature of the reports presented in Part A of this case as an example of what was available and commented on the fragmentation of the reports. After going over all the reports, Dr. Garrison responded, "There seems to be a lot of data here, but not much information." "Exactly," agreed Mr. Harris. "What we have doesn't seem to be very usable. That is why we want your help."

"Let me give you a little more background," Davis continued. "Not too long ago the marketing managers in our company met to discuss how we ought to go about building a good marketing information system for our company, but they couldn't agree on how to go about it. So, these senior managers decided that we ought to seek outside help in getting our marketing information system. Since my boss was most interested in the project, they charged him with finding a consultant. He turned the project over to me and, because of your company's reputation, here we are."

At this point, Professor Williamson asked a few questions. First, he wanted to know who the new information systems would serve. He was informed that it would be primarily used by top marketing management, but also by regional, zone, and territorial marketing managers, by market research, and by market planning. He also learned that product prices were set centrally and applied on a national basis.   Similarly, all advertising (mainly in trade publications) was handled nationally.   The company's marketing organization (in slightly more detail than in Part A) is shown below.

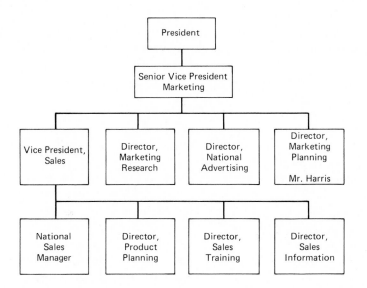

After the meeting concluded, Dr. Garrison and Professor Williamson met in Garrison's office to discuss the situation.   Garrison spoke first.   "You know Rudy, this situation seems to be an ideal one in which to come up with a good information systems design and at the same time adopt a strategy that will enhance user acceptance."

"Right," agreed Williamson.   "If we can facilitate the proper design process and see that a very successful system is produced, the opportunities for other related marketing information systems are limitless.   I hadn't thought of it before, but I had a call last Friday from the Antebellum Corporation (a division of a very large corporation located in Atlanta) that sounds like it has virtually the same problem.   If we can come up with a good procedure for doing a broad systems design for these sorts of marketing systems, we may have a great entrepreneurial opportunity."

ASSIGNMENT

1. You were not told what next step was recommended by Dr. Garrison and Professor Williamson at the conclusion of the first meeting. What specific next step do you think should have been recommended? Be specific, and detail the nature of the first step.

2. In their conversation after the meeting, Garrison and Williamson implied a design strategy coupled with gaining user acceptance. Outline, specifically, what steps would be taken to achieve a superior systems design and at the same time facilitate user acceptance. In other words, specify the design process and what specific features it would have that would be aimed at gaining user acceptance.

3. Does the strategy you recommend look anything like those listed or added in responding to the assignment in Part A of this case? What, if anything, is different, and why?

4. Discuss how the systems design procedure referred to at the end of the case, which Garrison sees as a great business opportunity, might look. Play the role of a consulting company that would market a "process" for developing marketing information systems. What would the key features of this process be (they should relate to your response to question 2)?

Tennison Petroleum is an oil exploration firm, headquartered in Houston, Texas. The company is only 15 years old. However, it has grown into an $800-million-per-year firm because of its phenomenal success in offshore drilling. Most of the success is attributed to their young, talented geophysical staff.

Tennison's phenomenal growth has increased the pressure to develop a good administrative support system. Most of its support services, such as personnel, computing services, and legal services, have been contracted outside of Tennison Petroleum. Their Big Eight accounting firm, during their recent audit, indicated that Tennison should move these services in-house, including developing its own information systems department.

The vice president of finance is charged with establishing the in-house information systems department, and begins a national search using an executive search firm to locate and hire a qualified information systems manager. After an extensive search, Tennison recruits Mike Parks, an experienced information systems manager.

Mike Parks has been in information systems for approximately 12 years. He started out as an accountant and moved into computer programming, systems analysis and design, and information systems management. All of his experience was with two other petroleum companies.

During the interview Sal March, the vice president of finance, arranges for Mr. Parks to meet with Mr. Tom Dock, president and founder of Tennison Petroleum. During that visit, Mr. Dock asks Mr. Parks where he thinks the information systems effort should report within Tennison Petroleum. Mr. Parks feels the best reporting relationship is into the president's office or to an executive vice president (which doesn't happen to exist at Tennison Petroleum). However, he is reluctant to state his views since Mr. March, the vice president of finance, seems to be controlling the hiring decision. Consequently, Mr. Parks states there are different views on the reporting relationships and indicates some of the pros and cons of having information systems report to different locations, such as the vice president of finance, a steering committee, or the president's office.

Mr. Dock asks Mr. Parks to whom he reports in his current position with the other petroleum company. Mr. Parks indicates that he reports to the vice president of finance.

Mr. Dock asks how that relationship has worked out for him. Mr. Parks indicates that it has been a very acceptable working relationship because the vice president of finance is more than fair in dealing with him and helping him allocate limited information systems resources.

Mr. Dock indicates that Mr. March feels fairly strongly about having information systems report in to him and that since Mr. Parks hasn't really experienced any problem with that type of reporting relationship in the past, he thinks he'd like to keep it that way. At that point, Mr. Dock offers the position of director of information systems to Mr. Parks at $10,000 more a year than Mr. Parks was expecting. Mr. Parks indicates that he'd like to think about the position and give him an answer the first of next week. Mr. Dock agrees to this, and after a brief meeting with Mr. March, Mr. Parks leaves.

The following week Mr. Parks accepts the offer and goes to work the following month as the director of information systems for Tennison Petroleum Company.

The Big Eight accounting firm had recommended that Tennison Petroleum establish a steering committee to set policies and priorities for information systems. Mr. March had established a steering committee prior to Mr. Parks accepting the position. During the early meetings with the steering committee, it became quite apparent there was quite a bit of controversy over what projects should be worked on first. After some rather painful and heated discussions, the steering committee came up with the following ranking of projects:

1. Develop a seismic analysis system.
2. Institute a materials requirement system for drilling projects.
3. Rework the accounts payable system.
4. Develop a contract system.
5. Create personnel and skills inventory system.

All other projects were deferred for consideration until next year. The ranking is agreed upon and signed off by all participants of the steering committee.

Three days after the steering committee meeting, Mr. March called a meeting with Mr. Parks. During the meeting, Mr. March indicated that he was very disappointed with the rankings that the steering committee came up with and did not feel that they were really consistent with the needs of the organization. Specifically, he felt that the budget system and payroll system needed much more attention than the committee was willing to recognize. Accordingly, he was going to alter the priorities and wanted Mr. Parks to ask his staff to begin work on the payroll and budgeting system.

Mr. Parks indicated he thought that might create a problem for them in that they had indicated to the steering committee that they would honor the priorities they had established. To deviate from that priority at all could cause a serious integrity problem, resulting in deterioration of the relationship between information systems and the steering committee.

Mr. March indicated he wasn't concerned about that. He said he knew what was best for the organization and that there was always a tendency among the nonfinancial people on steering committees to take financial systems for granted until they weren't there. The financial projects that he identified needed to be worked on.

Mr. Parks became very concerned that this could result in some serious political problems and reiterated his concerns to Mr. March. At that point Mr. March became impatient with Mr. Parks' arguments and indicated that the projects would be worked on in the order that Mr. March thought they should be worked on and that would be the end of it.

Mr. Parks suggested that in fairness to the committee members, they should be informed of the change in the priorities.

At that point Mr. March became very irritated and said that the committee didn't need to know about every decision that was made pertaining to information systems. He said they would work on the other projects, but they would just slow down the effort a little bit so they could fit in the financial systems of payroll and budget concurrent with working on the other projects.

After the meeting, Mr. Parks became very concerned about his situation. He realized that information systems reporting to the financial vice president created a conflict of interest and that one of his primary users was also his boss. The vice president of finance that he reported to in his previous organization had always gone out of his way to make sure no one could criticize him of serving his own interests first. But he realized with Mr. March, that would not be the case.

He waited a few days and, during a routine conversation with Mr. March, casually raised the issue again, but was quickly shut off and no opportunity was given for further discussion.

During the following couple of weeks, different people from the steering committee dropped by to check and see how things were going and indicated that they appreciated the participative approach that had been used to set priorities and were looking forward to the information systems that would be developed.

Mr. Parks becomes very concerned that he is going to be caught in a difficult ethical situation if he works on the financial projects, and it becomes known in the organization. On the other hand, he feels that he can't go against his boss who has taken a fairly firm stand.

Late that week, Mr. Dock invites Mr. Parks to join him for lunch. During the lunch, Mr. Dock just indicates a general interest to see how things are going. Mr. Parks sees the opportunity to subtly raise the issue of reporting relationships of information systems and goes over the pros and cons again, particularly emphasizing the con of the potential conflict of interest of having information systems report to finance. In so doing, he's hoping that Mr. Dock might pick up on the problem with Mr. March.

Mr. Dock misses the cue completely, or at least apparently misses the cue and responds, "Well, I'm glad we got that reporting relationship resolved before you started here and as you said, you were able to make it work in your previous job. I'm sure you can make it work."

ASSIGNMENT

1. What would you suggest Mr. Parks do in this delicate political situation?
2. In retrospect, are there things that Mr. Parks could have done differently during the job interview? What would they have been?